Fall

by **Bridget Carpenter**

SAMUEL FRENCH

FOUNDED 1830

NEW YORK HOLLYWOOD LONDON TORONTO

SAMUELFRENCH.COM

ISBN 978-0-573-66324-6   Printed in U.S.A.   #8221

MUSIC NOTE

Licensees are solely responsible for obtaining formal written permission from copyright owners to use copyrighted music in the performance of this play and are strongly cautioned to do so. If no such permission is obtained by the licensee, then the licensee must use only original music that the licensee owns and controls. Licensees are solely responsible and liable for all music clearances and shall indemnify the copyright owners of the play and their licensing agent, Samuel French, Inc., against any costs, expenses, losses and liabilities arising from the use of music by licensees.

IMPORTANT BILLING AND CREDIT
REQUIREMENTS

All producers of *FALL must* give credit to the Author of the Play in all programs distributed in connection with performances of the Play, and in all instances in which the title of the Play appears for the purposes of advertising, publicizing or otherwise exploiting the Play and/or a production. The name of the Author *must* appear on a separate line on which no other name appears, immediately following the title and *must* appear in size of type not less than fifty percent of the size of the title type.

In addition the following credit *must* be given in all programs and publicity information distributed in association with this piece:

The world premiere of "Fall" was produced by Trinity Repertory Company in May 2000. Oskar Eustis, Artistic Director, William P. Wingate, Managing Director

CHARACTERS

LYDIA, 14
JILL, 34
DOG, 44
GOPAL, 24
MR. GONZALES, 24
LEAD
FOLLOW

TIME

Late summer. The present.

PLACE

Southern California

SETTING

Outside, inside, around and about an enormous ballroom built in 1920. It overlooks the sea.

We can hear the crash of the ocean far below. The tops of palm trees may be visible, as the ballroom is several stories above sea level.

There is a bench, and plenty of room on the landing to dance.

Open French doors allow music from the ballroom to be heard.

There is a high wall which the sun hits just right at a certain time of day and it seems to invite you to perch on its wide ledge.

There is a wide-open camp feel.

CHARACTER NOTES

Lead and Follow are non-speaking roles. They are *superb* swing dancers, to be used in transitions and the background of many scenes.

Jill is sexy and wears cute clothes.

Gopal's parents are from India. Everyone is from California. People speak with a standard American accent, whatever that means.

DANCE NOTES

"Swing" is a general term – an umbrella designation for many specific dances: Lindy Hop, East Coast Swing, West Coast Swing, Shag, Balboa, the Big Apple, to name a few.

"Lindy Hop" is a specific dance. There are times I have used "lindy" as a verb (i.e., "Lead & Follow lindy through the room") and where this occurs, I envision the dancers doing a version of lindy hop, rather than 6-count swing.

The actors in this play do not have to be professional dancers (that's why Lead and Follow are there.) But actors should understand the rudiments of moving in rhythm.

Please, please: if you are producing this play: learn about the Lindy Hop. Watch videos of Frankie Manning, father of the Lindy Hop and originator of the aerial. Learn the steps to the Shim Sham. Hire wonderful Lindy Hoppers who are savvy swing dancers and can demonstrate style to the actors. And above all, be brave: go out swing dancing; observe – and partner with – as many dancers as possible in order to get a sense of the wide range of dance styles.

MUSIC NOTES

Scene titles are often songs which I was listening to when I wrote the scene, thus, something from the song may have found its way onto the page. It is not essential (indeed, it's inadvisable) to use the particular song to underscore the scene in production.

Exquisite, exuberant, joyous period swing music and dance is essential to this world. At times movement and music may take over. Actors might keep in mind that swing should be easy like breath.

THANK YOU:

FALL was written during a Princess Grace Fellowship in residence at New Dramatists in New York City.

Innumerable thanks go to Daniel Alexander Jones and Maria Mileaf, my first, priceless readers. To Cindy Geiger, swing instructor extraordinaire, and Lindy Bruce Moreira, erstwhile partner in the midwest. To Julie-Anne Robinson, who hosted me in London while I completed *FALL* and who put together a reading the day after I finished it. To Mimi Kilgore and the generous patrons of the Susan Smith Blackburn Award. And to the fine actors who read *FALL* and gave feedback during its development.

Most importantly, thanks to all my dance partners: from Tapestry, Mario's, Jitterbugs, the 100 Club, Irving Plaza, Swing 46, and many, many more; I was listening, every moment, every breath. Thank you.

You're walking. And you don't always realize it,
but you're always falling.
With each step, you fall forward slightly.
And then you catch yourself from falling.
Over and over, you're falling.

– Laurie Anderson
  Walking & Falling

scene 1
honeysuckle rose

(Ella Fitzgerald's version of "Honeysuckle Rose," or a song in a similar style*, plays.

JILL *stands in a suburban bedroom, packing clothes in a suitcase.*

She seems not to hear the music.

But

Once the horns kick in, she does a break that shows she's been listening all along. Now her movements are in perfect time. She adds a little footwork, nice and easy.

She hears a noise, looks up: it's **DOG**, *he's thrown his jacket aside and is holding out his arms. Like a musical.*

One jump, and they're together in perfect time.

They do a respectable 6-count swing, the occasional fancy move thrown in – maybe Jill's a little better than Dog. They look good together. They dance a while.

Lights come up on **LYDIA**, *separate.)*

LYDIA. *(calling)* Jill! *Jill!*

(Throughout the following conversation, **JILL** *and* **DOG** *dance.)*

JILL. Are you all packed, honey?
(to **DOG***)* You know why she's calling me by my first name now? Because she knows I hate it.

LYDIA. *(calling)* I'm not going!

DOG. We talked about this Lydia, you are too going.

LYDIA. I have scuba lessons! I can't miss them!

JILL. *(calling)* They have scuba instruction there, I checked.
(to Dog) She's mad at me.

*Please see Music Use Note on page 3.

9

DOG. At you? Her mother? No.

LYDIA. This camp will make me miss the first TWO DAYS of Fall term of my *freshman year,* Jill! That's socially handicapping me for life.

JILL. I'll write you a note.

LYDIA. Explaining that I'm not in school because I had to *swing.* With my *parents.* That'll get me in with Kool and the Gang. Let's just tattoo "winner!" on my forehead.

DOG. *(dancing)* It's family camp, Lids. We're a family.

LYDIA. *(calling)* We're not the *Partridge* family! I don't want to learn your stupid dance so we can take an act on the road!

DOG. *(to Jill)* Now there's a thought. She could play a tambourine. Lids, come on in here! Dance with your old man!

LYDIA. No way, Dad.

JILL. She calls you 'dad.' I don't get it.

DOG. I'll teach you a step...

LYDIA. I. DON'T. WANT. TO. GO. TO. SWING. CAMP! *God*! Three weeks OF SWING. It's like you *want* me to be an outcast.

JILL. Three weeks on a family vacation, and you'll miss two days of school. It happens all the time.

LYDIA. Why aren't you two into the Grateful Dead like normal people your age?

JILL. *(gritting teeth)* It's going to be fun, Lydia!

DOG. *(calling)* That's right, sweetie! You're going to have fun with your mother and me if we have to beat it into you with a stick!

LYDIA. When did you lose your connection to your own people?

JILL. Mr. and Mrs. Gonzales are going to be there.

LYDIA. Those are *your* friends!

JILL. The Gonzales' have a little girl, remember? You like Nina.

LYDIA. Jill. She's Five. I'm fourteen. Are you smoking crack again?

JILL. Don't ask if I'm smoking crack!

   (She stops dancing to talk to LYDIA.)

DOG. (Oh, here it comes.)

   (LYDIA sees her mother and starts to laugh.)

JILL. What is with you.

LYDIA. Nothing, Aunt Jemima. Can I have some pancakes?

JILL. OK! That talk is unacceptable!

LYDIA. What talk? I'm making an observation.

JILL. A racist observation!

LYDIA. It's not racist, it's astute.

JILL. You are being disparaging and disrespectful.

LYDIA. *(giggling)* What do you want me to call you, Rosie the Riveter?

JILL. I want you to call me Mom. Why are you always behaving this way to me?

LYDIA. Why are you always doing things for yourself, and pretending it's for me, when it's not?

JILL. This camp is for *all* of us.

LYDIA. Sorry I'm not the flawless dancing daughter you want.

JILL. I want my flawless daughter to *pack.*

LYDIA. I'm not going!

   (The final straw.)

JILL. You are going to Swing Camp with your father and me. This is our Family Time. Don't fuck with Family Time. Is that clear?

LYDIA. You. Are Ruining. My Life.

   (Lights out on LYDIA. DOG checks his watch.)

DOG. Refresh my memory. She's 14?

JILL. Last I checked.

DOG. So we're right on time.

   (The bedroom scatters.

   The ballroom becomes apparent.)

scene 2
the bends

LYDIA. There was this scuba documentary. And this diver got the bends. His tank was empty – he panicked – he had to release his weights. Too fast. Too fast. He fell up – through schools of silver fish – he fell towards the sky.

There are two parts to the bends. There are the Rushes, which means nitrogen bubbles have gotten in your blood. Rushes are not fatal, but you feel prickly, like ants are crawling on your skin. My scuba teacher said it's sort of horrible and exciting at the same time.

But. Full-on bends. Are different. Nitrogen is no longer just in your blood – it's now in your joints and in your muscle tissues, and it's like you've shaken up a can of coke and pricked it with a pin and the whole thing explodes.

That is what happens to your body. It is fucked up.

Know why they call it the bends? Cause when it happens to you, you bend.

(She clutches her stomach and bends over to demonstrate. Straightens up.)

The only sex I've ever had, and it wasn't really even sex, is the night my grandmother died, I went over to Julie-Anne Mariano's house, and we were all sitting there in the dark watching Saturday Night Live and pretending to drink Coors Light, and Sleazy Joe Rotella put his arm around me and sort of tried to make out, but I didn't want to. So he took my hand, and kissed my palm. And then for about a half hour he sort of sucked on my fingers.

It was interesting.

Because I didn't like Sleazy Joe at all, I still don't, but I felt sad because of my grandmother, and at the same time my stomach was jumpy and excited.

Julie-Anne has had sex with four people since seventh

grade. She says it's no big deal but if it's no big deal then why does she talk about it every day of our whole lives? Every day. Blah-blah-blah-I-slept-with-four-guys. I'm all, *I know.* Jesus.

Julie-Anne says she had sex with those four guys because each time she fell in love.

I cannot believe I have to go to Swing Camp.

scene 3
walk right in (walk right out)

(**GOPAL** *sits at a registration desk outside the ballroom, shuffling papers.* **JILL**, **DOG**, *and* **LYDIA** *stand with bags. Music plays over a creaky P.A. System.*)

DOG. *(to* **JILL***)* …I had wings, and you didn't know who I was.

JILL. *(to* **GOPAL***)* It's "Joss" …J-O-S-S.

DOG. I said, "Jill, Jill – you can't resist me – let's dance" and you said, "I don't dance with strangers." And then I was at my desk, and the wings were gone, and so were all my papers.

JILL. Your dream ends up in the office.

GOPAL. Here's a map to the campsite.

DOG. …You were there, too.

LYDIA. Is this music playing All The Time?

JILL. Zip it, Lydia.

LYDIA. Like the Twilight Zone.

DOG. *(listening)* I love this song.

LYDIA. You would.

DOG. You know, this is a famous ballroom. Movie stars used to come to this island.

LYDIA. *(looking around)* Children of the Corn. Children of the Swing.

GOPAL. You don't like to dance?

JILL.	**LYDIA.**
She's never tried.	You got it.

GOPAL. What's your name?

LYDIA. I don't remember. My mom hits me a lot, so I forget things.

JILL. *Lydia.*

(**GOPAL** *looks on his clipboard.*)

GOPAL. Lydia. So you are Jill and…Dog. – Oh I'm sorry, this must be a typo–

LYDIA. No, my dad was switched at birth with a German Shepherd.

JILL. Please excuse Lydia's bad manners. I'm Jill – you have it right – this is my husband Dog.

LYDIA. His name is Doug, but nobody calls him that. Because that would be too normal.

GOPAL. I'm Gopal.

LYDIA. *Gopal.* What's *that* mean?

GOPAL. Loosely translated, it means 'cowboy.'

LYDIA. How about tightly translated.

GOPAL. Herder of Cows.

(**DOG** *laughs.*)

LYDIA. You expect me to fall for that?

GOPAL. Everybody falls for something.

(**MR. GONZALES** *has arrived.*)

DOG. Heyyy – it's the young Jack Gonzales.

MR. GONZALES. Hi Dog. Jill.

JILL. Jack. Lydia, say hello to Mr. Gonzales.

LYDIA. Hello to Mr. Gonzales.

MR. GONZALES. Hi, Lydia.

(*Tousles her hair. She moves away.*)

JILL. She's in a rotten mood, don't pay any attention.

LYDIA. Isn't it weird, we only pay attention to the *good* moods? It seems unfair to leave all the other moods out. That must be why they're so pissy.

JILL. (*to* **JACK**, *pretending not to hear Lydia*) Isn't this beautiful?

DOG. Hey, Jack, where's everybody else??

MR. GONZALES. Michelle and Nina are home. They – decided not to come.

DOG. Oh.

JILL. Oh.

LYDIA. What's up with *that.*

JILL. Lydia!

MR. GONZALES. I thought – you know – why waste the reservations–

DOG. Sure! You can take home a new move!

JACK. *(to* **GOPAL***)* So it's just me.

GOPAL. Gonzales…here you go…and cross off…

JACK. Michelle. And Nina. Right.

GOPAL. O-kay. And swing passports for everybody!

(**GOPAL** *gives* **JILL, DOG, MR. GONZALES** *and* **LYDIA** *tags which they cheerfully place around their necks.*

LYDIA *holds her neck-tag out, staring at it in disbelief.*)

LYDIA. Swing Passports. I was wrong. This camp *is* cool.

(**JILL** *pretends deafness.*)

GOPAL. You guys are all set. The next session isn't 'til 3:30.

JILL. Lydia, why don't you register for your classes with Gopal, and Dog and I will go and explore camp.

LYDIA. *(withering)* Neat.

DOG. See you, kiddo!

(*to* **JACK***)* Why don't you follow us–

MR. GONZALES. …Okay.

(*They exit.*

LYDIA *looks steadily at* **GOPAL***.*)

LYDIA. So you're a swing kid?

GOPAL. Mm. I guess so.

(**LYDIA** *sighs heavily.*)

LYDIA. You live here on this island: you are surrounded by the best diving ever: you *swing*. God. Have you ever gone scuba diving?

GOPAL. I teach scuba.

(*Rest.*)

LYDIA. No way.

GOPAL. Sure.

LYDIA. You teach scuba here.

GOPAL. Well, I'm teaching dance this month, but usually, yeah.

LYDIA. You're *certified.*

GOPAL. Yeah.

LYDIA. Oh. ...Why would you teach swing instead of scuba?

GOPAL. You can't be underwater all the time.

LYDIA. I wish.

...My parents practice swing all the time. All the time. Every day.

GOPAL. I guess they want to be good.

LYDIA. I guess they want to be freaks.

(**GOPAL** *looks over some papers.*)

LYDIA. Have you heard of spontaneous combustion?

GOPAL. I think so.

LYDIA. My friend Julie-Anne told me about this girl who got out of the pool and burst into flame. In thirty seconds she was a pile of ashes.

GOPAL. Right out of the pool, huh.

LYDIA. I read about it. Spontaneous combustion. It happens. Do you even know what it's like, being stranded here with your *parents?*

GOPAL. Yeah. I do. My family runs this place.

LYDIA. Chh. So how does it make you feel?

GOPAL. Useful.

LYDIA. Well it makes me feel invisible. Transparent. Like water.

GOPAL. But you're not.

(*Rest.*)

LYDIA. So what dance classes should I take.

GOPAL. What do you want to take?

LYDIA. I *want* to take scuba, but that's only once a week.

GOPAL. How about beginning Lindy Hop?

(**LYDIA** *covers her face with her hands for a moment, horrified.*)

LYDIA. This embarrasses me just to talk about. It is *so severely lame.*

(At this moment, the **LEAD** *and* **FOLLOW** *dance through. Clearly, they have been practicing for a long time. They glide through the registration area, doing the Lindy Hop gorgeously together.*

LYDIA *and* **GOPAL** *watch them – the* **LEAD** *and* **FOLLOW** *are oblivious to everything but their own steps.*

After a wonderful episode of dance, they dance out.)

LYDIA. Was that Lindy Hop?

GOPAL. Yeah.

LYDIA. Fine. Sign me up for that.

GOPAL. *(smiling)* Okay.

LYDIA. Just cause I have no idea what else to put down.

GOPAL. Right.

LYDIA. I still think it's lame.

GOPAL. Oh, I know.

(Music comes from the P.A. System, and a voice:)

P.A. VOICE. *Those who have registered, come to the ballroom for an intermediate workshop in the Balboa!*

(**LYDIA** *puts her head in her hands again.)*

scene 4

*(**LYDIA** and **DOG** sit together. After a lesson.)*

DOG. That was good, huh?

   You did great, Lids.

LYDIA. You're such a bad liar, Dad.

DOG. Well. You *will* do great. It was just the first one. There's a lot more to come.

LYDIA. Goody gumdrops from the gumdrop tree.

   Look, there's that guy Attilla. He was my partner today.

   HEY ATTILLA!

   (She waves.)

DOG. *(hopefully)* Good partner?

LYDIA. He writes science fiction as a *hobby*. Why not just say the words, "I'm an asocial weenie" and be done with it?

DOG. You might tone down the sarcasm, Lids, just for variety's sake.

LYDIA. I dance for an hour with a guy named Attilla and I can't say anything? Get real.

DOG. *(sigh)*

LYDIA. Are you and Jill going to break up?

DOG. Lydia WHY do you keep asking that? Your mother and I love each other very much. We love you very much. We're all here together, and we are going to stay here together. WHAT have we done to make you think we're breaking up?

LYDIA. Nothing. Just if it happens, I don't want to be surprised. *(Rest)* Everything is about sex.

DOG. Ah, I don't think I caught that segue, honey.

LYDIA. It *is*. Sex, sex, sex, sex, sex, sex, sex, sex, sex, sex, sex, sex, sex, sex, sex, sex, sex, sex, sex, sex, sex, sex. It's everywhere. It's disturbing.

   *(**DOG** is fairly uncomfortable.)*

DOG. Lydia. honey. is there something you want to talk about? Because–

LYDIA. It's everywhere, you know, "SEX" – I just think it's *twisted* and I'm sick of it. All my friends especially Julie-Anne have this never-ending assessment of guys, this *debate* about whacking off, and whether it's just boys who do that, or whether *everybody* does it, or if we all just *think* about it, sex sex sex sex–

DOG. I get it.

(Rest)

LYDIA. I have my period. That's why I'm so moody.

*(**DOG** gets more uncomfortable but tries to deal with it.)*

DOG. Oh. Well. We can tell your mother and–

LYDIA. I've had my period for the last four years. Has Jill told you that?

DOG. *(momentarily shocked)* What?

LYDIA. I've been bleeding for four years. I mean bleeding every single day. "It'll stop soon," Jill told me. *Four years* without a break! Then I read that constant bleeding over several years often leads to spontaneous combustion–

(O.K., now he's pissed.)

DOG. *(angry) That is enough young lady.*

LYDIA. I'm going to turn into a pile of ashes!

DOG. You want to be a moody teenager: fine. That's what I see. You want me to quit being understanding? Cause I can just be "Dad" – you know, the dad you *want*, the dummy who doesn't get anything.

*(**LYDIA** and **DOG** look at one another. **LYDIA** looks repentant and sad. She leans forward, as though to impart a secret. **DOG** leans forward too.)*

LYDIA. Have you ever wished you had a vagina?

DOG. *(long exhalation of breath)*

(He gets up and exits.)

LYDIA. You think you see me, but you don't. You don't.

scene 5

(Dance class. **GOPAL** *stands in front of the audience.)*

GOPAL. What you want is a state of *light resistance.*

Face your partner.

Hold your hands up.

Now, the *leads* should *push* with one hand.

All right it's resistance not rigor mortis.

Mrs. Clyde, you need to allow your husband to lead you.

I'm sure that's unfamiliar.

Try again.

*(**GOPAL** watches. They're not good.)*

Mr. Chin, *light* resistance.

Light tension, Ethyl.

Tension plus Resistance equals Momentum.

(The **LEAD** *and* **FOLLOW** *come on. They dance slowly –* **LEAD** *pushes,* **FOLLOW** *spins.* **FOLLOW** *pushes,* **LEAD** *spins.*

They spin faster and faster until they are whirling in an arc and it is impossible to tell who is pushing who.)

scene 6
the devil & the deep blue sea

(Underwater.

Blue/green ocean light.

LYDIA *appears in snorkeling gear.*

She moves slowly, with wonder, reaching up to touch a fish.

LYDIA *swims very slowly, blissful in the ocean. She reaches down to pick up a conch shell and places it to her ear.*

There is the sound of swing music underwater.

LYDIA *hears this music.*

She tries to swim away from the music, but cannot.

She swims faster, faster; the music follows her as she goes.)

scene 7

(**LYDIA** *sits, legs dangling over the side of the wall. She wears a snorkeling mask and has a tube in her mouth.*

MR. GONZALES *approaches. He might be carrying a book, reading.*)

LYDIA. *(something unintelligible with her mouthpiece in.)*

(No response.)

LYDIA. *(something unintelligible with her mouthpiece in, LOUD-ER.)*

MR. GONZALES. So. Lydia. Hello.

(**LYDIA** *salutes.*)

MR. GONZALES. Are you practicing your scuba?

(**LYDIA** *looks at him in utter disbelief. How can any adult be so stupid. She removes the snorkel from her mouth.*)

LYDIA. *(slowly, as though to a child)* Well. First of all, this is snorkeling gear. Scuba requires a tank. Second, I'm not *in* the water. The ocean looks like it's, I don't know, five stories below. So no, I'm not practicing my *scuba.*

MR. GONZALES. I guess not.

LYDIA. How do you know my dad again? You're certainly not his *age.*

MR. GONZALES. I know your mom.

LYDIA. Uh huh.

MR. GONZALES. We work together. Teaching.

LYDIA. Uh huh.

You guys, like, hang out in the Faculty Room. Drinking Coffee.

MR. GONZALES. We're at the same school.

LYDIA. Uh huh.

That is incredibly illuminating.

(Long pause.)

LYDIA. Thinking some big thoughts, huh.

MR. GONZALES. Oh I don't know.

(*Long pause.*)

LYDIA. Query. Do you have anyone to talk to?
Like, do you actually say things. That are revealing.

MR. GONZALES. (*shrug*)

(**LYDIA** *waits.*)

LYDIA. Well nice talking with you, Mr. Gonzales.

(**LYDIA** *replaces the snorkel mouthpiece and stares out to sea.*)

scene 8

LYDIA. First scuba class today. First week. First ocean dive.

(**LYDIA** *beams with pleasure.*)

I fall towards the ocean floor, slow.

Quiet underwater. Just the sound of my heart.
Thick. Heavy.

There are hundreds of tiny fish around me, thousands.

I touch a spiny cucumber that feels like moss.

My teacher looks at me, and makes the sign 'OK' like 'are you OK' and I make the sign back. Because I am. OK.

I'm underwater. Jill's somewhere on the shore. No one sees me but the fish. I'm OK.

scene 9
I'm beginning to see the light

(Music. **GOPAL** *gives a private lesson to* **JILL** *and* **DOG***; he's demonstrating the opening stance of an aerial.)*

GOPAL. To begin with, Dog, your center of balance should be low.

JILL. Ooh, Dog, you're vibrating.

(Wait a minute.)

JILL. You're *vibrating.*

DOG. Excuse me! I'm swinging.

JILL. I don't believe you.

DOG. What! Oh, I completely forgot that was there.

*(***JILL*** has answered his cellphone.)*

JILL. Hello.
Yeah well he can't talk right now, he's dancing. Hi Karl.

DOG. Oh, geez–

JILL.	**DOG.**
Have you pitched a tent in the office?	Honey!
I bet that's neat.	

DOG. You see, she thinks this is funny.

JILL. No I don't. *(back to phone)* It must be fabulous there. At work. I mean why else would you call on someone's vacation?

*(***DOG*** grabs phone.)*

DOG. Karl?
Yeah, no, I'm sorry, what's up.
Well, you need to tell them that's unacceptable.

(He looks at **JILL***.)*

DOG. Karl, I've told you a thousand times, don't call me! I'm *dancing,* and *dancing comes first.* (Talk to you in an hour.)

(He hangs up theatrically.)

JILL. *(to* **GOPAL***)* Does this happen to you often? Do other people bring their *phones* to class?

DOG. Hello? I hung up!

JILL. You did, didn't you. I'm going to give you a cookie.

DOG. Well, good.

GOPAL. So Dog, you need to lead this combination from a strong base.

DOG. I'm not so sure about this aerial moves stuff…

JILL. You should try everything once.

DOG. *(muttering)* "…try everything once, except aerials and incest."

*(***JILL*** rolls her eyes.)*

GO3PAL. I think the saying is, you should try everything once, except for *incest* and *folk dancing.*

*(***JILL*** and* **GOPAL** *think this is funny.)*

DOG. Didn't I read somewhere about a guy killing his dance partner when he tried to flip her? Broke her neck.

JILL. Dog, don't be asinine.

DOG. I *read* something…

GOPAL. That was years ago.

JILL. *What?*

GOPAL. *Kidding,* I'm kidding. You two are going to be fine.

DOG. I don't think we're advanced enough for this, hon.

JILL. Come *on,* I want to learn aerials! That's what we came here for! Aerials!

DOG. What *you* came here for.

JILL. *(overlapping)*	**DOG.** *(overlapping)*
It's supposed to be a vacation, a VACATION, and you insist on being half here, half somewhere else, I mean really!	Just because I feel nervous about picking you up and tossing you around does not mean I'm not on vacation – I am here!

(**GOPAL** *is starting to get uncomfortable.*)

GOPAL. Now, to do aerials well, you have to trust your partner…

DOG. Maybe you want to find another partner. Mr. Leo maybe, you can trust him.

JILL. You are being such a *baby*! I want *you* to be my partner.

DOG. It's *advanced*. It says so in the brochure. Advanced.

JILL. We're advancing!

GOPAL. These particular dance moves are about balance and momentum, not force.

DOG. Tell *her*!

JILL. (Jesus.)

GOPAL. You'll be going at your own pace…

JILL. *(to Dog)* You have to attempt to *move* before you can pick a pace!

DOG. Hey. You know what Jill? *You* pick a pace. I'm out of here.

(*He stomps out.*)

JILL. *(calling off)* Where are you going!

DOG. *(from off)* Tap!

(**GOPAL** *and* **JILL** *are left in an awkward quiet.*)

GOPAL. Um. That's a good class, tap.

(*Rest*)

GOPAL. We can still work on some support basics.

JILL. You know why I wanted to learn aerials?

I want to be thrown Straight Up.

Some people dream about having wings, or about being lost, or about running away to the circus.

I dream about being swung out – swung up, and over, and letting go.

Because when you're in the air like that, you're not somebody's teacher, or somebody's wife, or somebody's mother. You're just – whssssshhhhh.

(*She closes her eyes.*)

scene 10

(The ballroom. Dance lighting. **LYDIA** *sits alone in a folding chair. Music.)*

P.A. VOICE. *...so find a partner, and welcome to swing camp's dance-o-rama!!*

*(***JILL*** *and* ***DOG*** *dance by, immersed in the music. They don't see* **LYDIA**. **MR. GONZALES** *approaches, stands by her, in his own world.*

LYDIA. Hi Mr. Gonzales.

MR. GONZALES. Lydia.

LYDIA. *(holds up her hand)*

MR. GONZALES. Is anyone sitting in this chair?

*(***LYDIA*** *gives a withering glance.*

*   **MR. GONZALES** *sits.)*

MR. GONZALES. You're not wearing your snorkeling gear.

LYDIA. (Jesus.)

*(***MR. GONZALES*** *sits. They don't talk for a moment. They watch people dance. One song ends – clapping, cheers from off – and another begins.)*

LYDIA. Mr. Gonzales. How come you're here alone?

MR. GONZALES. Well Lydia. Good question.

LYDIA. But no answer.

MR. GONZALES. *(shrugs)*

LYDIA. There you go again. Chatty.

(He looks at her. She looks away.)

MR. GONZALES. Some concept, isn't it.

LYDIA. What.

MR. GONZALES. Whole room full of men and women, all of them getting along.

LYDIA. Huh.

MR. GONZALES. I imagine your parents didn't consult you before they planned your summer vacation.

(A steady gaze from **LYDIA**.*)*

LYDIA. Are you trying to bond with me? Did my mother tell you to sit here?

MR. GONZALES. No.

LYDIA. You're gonna go dance, huh.

MR. GONZALES. Eventually.

LYDIA. How come you're not out there now?

(**MR. GONZALES** *doesn't know.*)

MR. GONZALES. …I'd rather talk. To you.

LYDIA. Oh.

MR. GONZALES. What did your friends say about swing camp.

LYDIA. You think I *told* people? Think again.

MR. GONZALES. No one's going to be a bit curious over your missing the first couple days of school?

LYDIA. I told everyone I was getting a nose job.

MR. GONZALES. But you have a beautiful nose.

LYDIA. Chh. I'm not *really* getting a nose job. That's just what I'm telling people.

(*She is secretly quite pleased at his statement.*)

LYDIA. Lots of people get nose jobs at my school.

MR. GONZALES. Maybe lots of people at your school need nose jobs but you're not one of them.

(*She successfully hides her smile.*)

LYDIA. Even if I did need one I wouldn't get it. Would you ever get one?

MR. GONZALES. Do you think I need one?

LYDIA. No.

MR. GONZALES. Whew. Good.

LYDIA. Don't make fun of me.

MR. GONZALES. I wasn't.

LYDIA. Okay.

MR. GONZALES. Okay.

(*They watch the dancers.*)

LYDIA. Do you ever think that swing dancing is like the revenge of the lames? Look at these people. Mr. Leo. Check out Mr. Leo.

(They watch **MR. LEO.***)*

MR. GONZALES. *(contemplative)* Mr. Leo can *swing*.

LYDIA. That's what I'm saying.

You see that guy over there? The eighty-four year old. Four feet tall.

MR. GONZALES. Dancing with the bald woman.

LYDIA. Right. That's Ethyl and Bob. They're from Lancaster: one vacation a year: Camp. This is a room filled with the most boring people alive.

MR. GONZALES. You dance with any of them?

LYDIA. No.

MR. GONZALES. Your mother can really–

LYDIA. Yeah I *know*.

MR. GONZALES. Hard to believe you're not up on your feet, too.

LYDIA. Nobody *asked*. *(beat)* Every person here dances better than me.

I am so bad. Look at them. They...I don't get, get how just – they're *themselves* and so awkward and so–

MR. GONZALES. Pure.

LYDIA. Yeah. They are.

You'd never know how boring they are. It changes.

When they start. The men just open their arms and the women fall. It's–

MR. GONZALES. Like a fairy tale.

LYDIA. Like that story about the twelve dancing princesses.

MR. GONZALES. Feet barely touching the ground.

(Both **LYDIA** *and* **MR. GONZALES** *lean forward, transfixed. Then the spell is broken.)*

LYDIA. It is so unfair. That I have to come here and watch them. Like it's not enough at home. They dance; I watch. Same old.

MR. GONZALES. It is unfair. I know exactly what you mean.

LYDIA. I'm invisible here.

It fucking sucks.

(DOG and JILL dance by again. DOG waves merrily at LYDIA.)

DOG. HI LIDS! *(Blows her a kiss)*

BYE LIDS!

LYDIA. He is so disturbing. Do you know how embarrassing it is to have a father who *swings?*

MR. GONZALES. Can't say that I do.

When I was fourteen, my father had me drink with him, man to man. And after a few beers, my father turned to me and said, I liked your mother better than you. That's all. And I, uh, didn't say anything.

(They watch the dancers.)

LYDIA. You know why I wouldn't ever get a nose job? Because I think it's important to like somebody *because* of their flaws. Not to *wait* until they're perfect. Not everything can be fixed. Not everybody learns how to dance.

MR. GONZALES. Not everybody tries.

LYDIA. *(a challenge)* I think my parents are going to break up.

(MR. GONZALES is taken aback but hides it.)

MR. GONZALES. What makes you think that?

LYDIA. I don't know. I just do.

(She goes back to watching the dancers, sneaking a glance at MR. GONZALES, who is watching JILL.)

LYDIA. *(pointedly)* You know if you're gonna ask my *mother* to dance, you should find her before the next break. She's a woman in *demand.*

MR. GONZALES. Maybe later.

(LYDIA looks away, shy.)

LYDIA. Have you ever gone scuba diving?

MR. GONZALES. No.

LYDIA. You'd like it.

(Dance music changes. Clapping from off)

MR. GONZALES. You gonna take me?

LYDIA. "Maybe later."

*(They sit companionably. **MR. GONZALES** stands up.)*

MR. GONZALES. Well. Why don't we give it a try.

(He touches her nose, holds out his arms.

LYDIA*: Internal freakout.)*

LYDIA. Um, no. Thank you.

scene 11

(**JILL** *and* **LYDIA** *sit in arts and crafts. They are concentrating hard on making candles in milk cartons.*)

P.A. VOICE. *Calling all swing kids: Wear your vintage finery to this week's dance and win a prize! And dancers, remember to give your feet a rest. If your dogs have been barking, take a break – you can weave a basket, throw a pot, and much more when you visit the craft hut!*

JILL. Right now the kids have finished their spelling tests... and they're lining up for recess...and there's a teacher counting heads...and it's *not me*. Isn't this great?

LYDIA. We swing...we make sand candles. This is the best vacation of my whole life.

JILL. Lydia, don't use so much sand.

LYDIA. (*disbelieving*) You're an expert *candlemaker*, too?

(**LYDIA** *begins to mutter to herself as* **JILL** *busies herself with her own candle.*)

LYDIA. I'm sorry that I missed the issue of *Martha Stewart Living* that had the Big Candlemaking Expose. Jesus. It's a sand candle, a five year-old could do it, I mean, what's next, a seminar on macrame? Or maybe if I'm lucky I'll win a prize for a pot holder!

(*Triumphant music swells over her words.* **LYDIA** *stares.*

Over a crackled and strange P.A. system we hear:)

P.A. VOICE. *And the Grand Jury First Prize for...Lydia, are you listening?*

LYDIA. (*unnerved*) What?

P.A. VOICE.	**LYDIA.**
The Grand Jury First Prize for Amazing Candlemaking goes to...JILL!	No. No!

(*We are now deep inside Lydia's fantasy.*

Sounds of applause, whistles, trumpets.

GOPAL *marches carrying a shiny, enormous, glittering candlemaking trophy that reads:*

JILL!

JILL's *hands fly to her face like the Miss America pageant winners who are like* "I don't believe it"

Music swells even louder.

JILL *accepts the trophy from* **GOPAL**.)

JILL. *(Mouthing soundlessly)* Thank you! *Thank you so much...*

(**DOG** *is behind* **GOPAL**, *carrying a garish banner that reads:*

1 CANDLEMAKER!

He waves it over **JILL**'s *head.*

JILL *clutches the trophy to her chest with emotion.* **GOPAL** *and* **DOG** *are applauding wildly.* **MR. GONZALES** *enters, applauding. He holds out his arms;* **JILL** *puts down the trophy, takes* **MR. GONZALES**' *hands and the two begin spinning in slow motion, like lovers in a meadow.* **LYDIA** *watches, aghast.*

Music shifts from 'triumphant' to 'romantic'

GOPAL *keeps applauding;* **DOG** *keeps waving the banner;* **JILL & MR. GONZALES** *keep whirling around and around wearing sappy expressions.*

Music shifts, gets a bit static perhaps...a voice can be heard under the music...)

P.A. VOICE. *And there is once again a Grand Jury Prize for best vintage costume, so start planing now. We want to see you hepcats dressed to the nines!*

(Things have returned to normal. **GOPAL, DOG, MR. GONZALES**, *and the candlemaking trophy are all gone.*

JILL *is intent on her candle.)*

JILL. ...I just think you want to have a wax-to-sand ratio that's higher on the wax...
Lydia? Something the matter?

LYDIA. ...it's just...those P.A. announcements are realy annoying. They're freaky.

(GOPAL enters)

GOPAL. Hey, Lydia.

JILL. Hm. If it's candles, it must be Tuesday.

Hi, Gopal.

LYDIA. It's Cowboy.

(He sits and begins knotting small pieces of plastic.)

JILL. You're not teaching right now?

GOPAL. My mom likes it when I help her out in arts and crafts.

JILL. See, some people help their mothers.

LYDIA. Yeah, Gopal is perfect. What are you making.

GOPAL. A lanyard.

LYDIA. And what is that.

GOPAL. …I don't know.

(He takes a key chain out of his pocket. There are perhaps 20 other lanyards on it. He adds his new one.)

JILL. God the air is different here. You probably don't notice – you're here all summer. So it doesn't feel 'different' to you. This is your normal. Lucky.

LYDIA. Chh. How long have you worked here?

GOPAL. Probably since I was your age.

LYDIA. Is there swing in India?

JILL. Lydia.

GOPAL. Don't know. Never been.

LYDIA. But your *parents* were born there.

GOPAL. Right.

LYDIA. And they came here to…swing? What is that about.

JILL. Lydia don't be rude.

LYDIA. I'm interested! I'm not being rude!

GOPAL. My folks came to California when they were still teenagers. My dad had this accounting job, really an amazing opportunity for an immigrant, but he was really lonely, homesick, ready to leave. One night they were out for a walk, and he was telling my mother that he couldn't take it, he was going to quit his job so they could go home. And they stopped inside this club to talk. And onstage…Ella Fitzgerald was singing, just sitting in with the band. My father says that when he heard her sing, he forgot his brothers and sisters. Forgot his parents and school friends. Forgot everything. He stopped talking, he took my mother's hand, and they watched everyone dance, listening to Ella.

He says her music was why they stayed.

LYDIA. That's cool.

Jill and Dog are breaking up.

JILL. We are not! Lydia, stop it!

LYDIA. I was just kidding.

JILL. It's not funny.

LYDIA. *(concentrating)* My candle is going to kick butt...

JILL. Lydia, honey, I do think you're using too much sand...

LYDIA. Jill, you make your candle, I'll make mine.

JILL. O-kay.

P.A. VOICE. *Come one come all – advanced east coast swing is taking place in five minutes at studio four!*

JILL. Oops – that's where I'm meeting Dog – Lydia, want to finish my candle?

LYDIA. Okay.

JILL. Bye, baby!

LYDIA. Happy swinging.

(JILL exits.)

GOPAL. These look ready to try – you want to go first?

LYDIA. Sure.

GOPAL. Let's see yours.

(LYDIA pulls her candle out of the milk carton by the wick. The wick is attached to nothing. She turns over the carton to dump out her candle, which is in fact a miniature pile of rubble.)

LYDIA. Well that sucked.

(GOPAL takes Jill's candle out of the milk carton by the wick. It is perfect. Stellar. A beautiful candle.

LYDIA *and* **GOPAL** *stare at the wondrous candle.)*

scene 12

(**LYDIA** *by herself, awkwardly practicing a dance step.*

Sometime during her practicing, **MR. GONZALES** *enters, holding a book.*)

LYDIA. (step step triple-step, step step triple-step)
(step step triple-step, step step triple-step)
(one two three-and-four, five six sevn-and-eight)
(one two three-and-)
– OH MY GOD.

(**LYDIA** *stops dancing immediately.*)

LYDIA. Hi.

MR. GONZALES. Hi.

LYDIA. Were you just watching me?

(**MR. GONZALES** *is settling in with his book.*)

MR. GONZALES. No.

LYDIA. Oh.

(**MR. GONZALES** *reads. Little moment.*)

MR. GONZALES. Falling right into the rhythm I see.

LYDIA. Hardly.
– You just said you weren't watching.

MR. GONZALES. I saw – this much.

(*He holds up his fingers in a pinch.*)

LYDIA. Oh.

(**MR. GONZALES** *returns to his book.*)

LYDIA. Were you in class this morning?

MR. GONZALES. Yes.

LYDIA. I didn't go.
Was it hard?

MR. GONZALES. I suppose it was pretty basic.

LYDIA. I didn't go because I can't stand being the worst one there.
It's exhausting.

MR. GONZALES. You want me to show you what we did?

LYDIA. No.

MR. GONZALES. Okay.

(*Rest*)

LYDIA. You don't seem to care about swing very much.

MR. GONZALES. Neither do you.

LYDIA. That's because I stink.

MR. GONZALES. I see.

(*He reads.* **LYDIA** *slumps in despair.*)

LYDIA. It's a special kind of hell to be crappy at something while everyone around you is wonderful.

MR. GONZALES. That's how I feel about parties.

LYDIA. What do you mean.

MR. GONZALES. Everyone likes to go to parties. I always feel uncomfortable.

(*He reads.*)

LYDIA. Well do you bring your *book* to parties?

MR. GONZALES. Do you think it would help?

LYDIA. *No.* Ha ha.

(*Rest*)

MR. GONZALES. You're sure you don't want me to teach you what learned this morning.

LYDIA. Pass.

MR. GONZALES. If I don't practice right away, it's like it never happened.

LYDIA. Um. Okay.

MR. GONZALES. It was something like–
Here–
Tuck, turn and back–

(*They try.*)

MR. GONZALES. Almost. Again.
Tuck, turn and back–

(**JILL** *has entered and is watching.*

LYDIA *missteps.*)

LYDIA. Sorry.

MR. GONZALES. No, it's me. See, I forgot the lead already.

(**LYDIA** *giggles.* **JILL** *steps in.*)

JILL. *(to Lydia)* Look at you!
Come here, you, I missed you in there. Let's cut a rug.

(She holds out her arms to her daughter. **LYDIA** *is appalled; maybe she recoils.)*

LYDIA. *Please.*

(As in, "Bitch, please.")

(Rest)

JILL. I think Lydia's going to be really good.

LYDIA. What could possibly lead you to draw that conclusion.

MR. GONZALES. I was showing Lydia what we learned in class this morning.

JILL. Oh, sweetie, you would have had fun. It's flashy.
(opening her arms to **MR. GONZALES**)
Here, show her the pinwheel–

*(***MR. GONZALES*** *glances at* **LYDIA**.)*

MR. GONZALES. You know: I think I just got a little foot cramp. I'm gonna stop for right now.

JILL. *(nonplussed, maybe)* Okay. – Lydia, want to come to a Smooth Lindy Workshop after lunch with your father and me?

LYDIA. Maybe. But I should go and round up my "swing homies" for practice.

MR. GONZALES. Sure, a bunch of us thick-headed ones are going to put in some time, really nail that footwork.

(He winks. **LYDIA** *hides a smile.)*

JILL. Well whatever you want. I'd love it if you came to the workshop.
See you later.

*(***JILL*** *exits.* **MR. GONZALES** *picks up his book.)*

MR. GONZALES. I think I'm going to go find a party, somewhere to read. Thanks for helping me practice.

(He exits.

LYDIA *watches him go.)*

scene 13
petootie pie

(*JILL and* DOG *sit in silence, holding cards.* JILL *discards, draws.*

DOG *looks at his hand.* JILL *clears her throat.* DOG *looks up, discards, draws. Both look at their hands.*

They play throughout their conversation, punctuating their words with the slap of cards.)

JILL. Did you talk to whats his name about the thing?

DOG. Mm hm. Worked out for now.

JILL. Good.

We should visit that couple.

DOG. They are nice.

JILL. When we get back.

DOG. Sure. We can go to that place, remember the time, after the long thing.

JILL. That's a good idea.

DOG. Ran into Jack this morning when you were at lindy stretch. Quiet guy.

JILL. I guess.

DOG. You think he feels odd here? Without his wife?

JILL. He hasn't talked about it.

I don't think he ever talked about her a lot, though. Even before.

DOG. That's a bad sign.

JILL. Why.

DOG. Because when you love someone, they come up.

(JILL *and* DOG *look at each other.*

LYDIA *enters.*)

LYDIA. It's the parents.

JILL. Gin.

DOG. I'm going to call, I gotta check in.

JILL. Yes you do.

DOG. Yes I do.

>   (**DOG** *kisses* **JILL** *on the forehead, she's shuffling the cards and doesn't look up.*)

DOG. Bye Lids.

LYDIA. Bye Dog.

DOG. *Backwards*, Lid…

LYDIA. Bye God.

>   (**DOG** *exits.*)

JILL. You want to play?

LYDIA. I guess.

>   (**JILL***: Surprise*)

JILL. *Great!* All right… here we go…

>   (**JILL** *shuffles and deals.*)

JILL. Did you have your scuba class with Gopal yet?

LYDIA. It's this lady instructor. Not Gopal.

JILL. Oh.

LYDIA. It's tomorrow.

JILL. Oh.

LYDIA. Gopal knows someone who spontaneously combusted. He said it started in her heart and spread like a forest fire. Instant ashes.

JILL. Well I'm sure it will be very nice. – OK!

LYDIA. Jill.

JILL. Mm Hm.

LYDIA. How did you meet dad?

>   (**JILL** *looks at* **LYDIA**. *This is new.*)

JILL. In college.

LYDIA. …You guys were not in college at the *same time*. What was he, your babysitter?

JILL. Ha ha. He was an instructor.

LYDIA. *(horrified and fascinated)* He Was Your Teacher?!

JILL. *No*, Lydia. A Visiting Instructor in the business school.

LYDIA. Did he give you an "A."

JILL. I didn't take his class. I was in education, and I had a friend in econ, and he introduced me to your father. We were friends.

LYDIA. *How* old were you?

JILL. Sophomore.

LYDIA. And how old was he.

JILL. He was 29, 30.

LYDIA. And you guys were friends. And then you stopped. Being friends.

JILL. He wanted to be more than friends.

LYDIA. And did you?

JILL. ...I wanted to be around your father all the time.

LYDIA. Why?

JILL. Because he was...so...happy.

He was the happiest person I'd ever met.

That's why everyone called him Dog.

LYDIA. *(amazed)* You got married while you were *still* in *school.*

JILL. We did. I was just 19.

It seems crazy now, but it made sense then. And then we had you, which was the best thing that ever happened to either of us.

LYDIA. Did Grandma and Grandpa freak out?

JILL. They were a little worried about the age difference at first. But then they met him. And saw what a...decent human being he was. Is. Everything worked out.

Things work out when you fall in love.

LYDIA. So after you stopped being friends...

JILL. We didn't *stop* being friends.

LYDIA. Ch. You got *married.*

JILL. And we're *friends.*

LYDIA. Whatever. So you say.

JILL. Yes, I say. And Lydia – you don't judge your father and me.

LYDIA. I'm not judging! I'm just asking!

JILL. Okay. Your discard.

> (*They play.*)

LYDIA. So are you and Dad monogamous?

JILL. What kind of a question is that?

LYDIA. Julie-Anne's parents have an open marriage.

JILL. You're kidding.

LYDIA. That's what her mom said.

JILL. Really.

LYDIA. Because Julie-Anne's father has a girlfriend. It's no big deal.

JILL. Ah, yes it is.

LYDIA. So does Dad have a girlfriend?

JILL. No.

LYDIA. If he did would you guys break up?

JILL. No, we wouldn't.

LYDIA. So it's no big deal.

JILL. We wouldn't break up, but it doesn't mean it's not a big deal.

   You make choices in a relationship. Nobody is perfect. People make mistakes. And when that happens, you make a decision to forgive them, and you move forward.

LYDIA. Has Dad made mistakes?

JILL. No.

LYDIA. Have you?

JILL. …Yes.

LYDIA. (whoa.)

> (**LYDIA** *decides not to pursue this.*)

JILL. Your father is my other half. I don't know who I'd be without him. Or you. I wouldn't be myself.

   And…that's all I'm going to say.

> (*They play.*)

LYDIA. So did you "know" right away that he was the one? When you met Dad?

JILL. Not right away. But there was a moment. And then I knew.

LYDIA. Tss. But how did you know?

How do you know it wasn't just random, like he could have been talking to *anybody* and it didn't mean anything and it just happened to be you. An accident.

JILL. Oh, honey. You just – you know, people talk. Men and women. And someone will be talking. And suddenly you'll know that they're *really* talking to you. Saying something to you they couldn't say to anyone else. And it's very special – that connection.

That's how you know.

(They play.)

LYDIA. Cards are stupid. I'm going to go make a lanyard.

(She exits.)

scene 14

GOPAL. When you hold your partner, You don't grip. You don't clench. You don't wring the life out of the hands.

It's a shared endeavor.

So you hold one another appropriately.

(A question from the class.)

It means appropriately, Mr. Peterson.

(A question from the class.)

Well, passion is not something that fuels swing. If you want passion go to Tango Camp.

(A question from the class.)

In October.

scene 15

(**MR. GONZALES** *sits, legs over the side of the wall, lost in thought.*)

LYDIA. Hi, Mr. Gonzales...

Hi, Mr. Gonzales.

MR. GONZALES. Lydia. You can call me Jack.

LYDIA. Okay. Jack. What are you doing.

MR. GONZALES. Just thinking.

LYDIA. What are you thinking about.

MR. GONZALES. This beach reminds me of – someplace else.

LYDIA. What kind of name is 'Jack Gonzales.'

MR. GONZALES. An American name.

LYDIA. But are you from Mexico?

MR. GONZALES. No.

LYDIA. Do you speak Spanish?

MR. GONZALES. No.

LYDIA. How come?

MR. GONZALES. My father didn't want me to.

LYDIA. Oh.

MR. GONZALES. "Speak English, be American." So I did. I spoke English. I spoke English, I went to Yale, I majored in education, I had a daughter, I married a girl from Connecticut. Not the right order, but...Just like my father wanted.

LYDIA. What about your mother?

MR. GONZALES. She's dead.

LYDIA. Sorry.

MR. GONZALES. Don't be. You didn't kill her.

(*Rest.*)

LYDIA. Was it recent?

MR. GONZALES. No, no. When I was little. Five.

LYDIA. Do you remember her?

MR. GONZALES. A bit.

LYDIA. Do you miss her?

MR. GONZALES. Questions. Questions.

LYDIA. *(hurt)* Sor-ry.

Forgive me for thinking you might want to talk. To me. My mistake.

(Silence)

MR. GONZALES. When I was five, my mother, my father and me came here to the seaside. A picnic. My mother had made little cakes and I had brought a kite which didn't fly. There was a balloon. The kind you ride in. Dollar a ride. My mother wanted to go. Not my Dad. And I was too little. So she got in the basket – and he stayed on the ground, holding my hand.

The sky was no color at all. We watched my mother go up, up, up. The balloon grew smaller and smaller as the wind pushed it above the low clouds. She was just a tiny…thing…in the basket. And I let go of my father's hand, I jumped up and down. I held my arms high in a V to her. I waved and waved. I wanted her to see me. And she waved back! She imitated me exactly, both arms high. And then…she was in the air. Arms still waving. I watched her fall. She was dark against the pale sky, a doll.

When I looked up at my father, his hair had turned white. And instead of running in the direction where she fell, he turned his back.

He never spoke my mother's name aloud again. He could not forgive her for leaning out too far. He could not forgive me for…And – why should he. Why should he.

(Silence)

LYDIA. Your mother, I bet she always wanted something. Something she couldn't name.

In the air – she saw her little boy. She looked down, and there you were: the person she loved most in the world. It must have felt so perfect. She had to raise her arms. Because she was happy. She wasn't holding you, but she *wanted* to. That's why she leaned into the sky. She couldn't contain her joy. Did you ever think of that?

scene 16

LYDIA. Second scuba class. Second week. Second ocean dive.

Today, we go deeper.

The surface of the sea is far above.

I could stay and stay down here in the perfect clear blue. Just me and the fish.

When we're back up on the deck of the boat, sitting in the warm air peeling off our wet suits, I can feel it happening to me.

Rushes. Rushes. Lightheaded, this feeling of buoyancy, dizzy in my stomach. Cold sweat. Fast heartbeat. Falling.

Rushes. I have to lie down, I can't talk.

At night alone in my cot, I close my eyes and I can still feel it, I can still feel everything.

I taste ashes on my tongue.

scene 17
is you is, or is you ain't (ma'baby)

(**DOG** *is dancing with* **JILL**. **GOPAL** *watches. They're having a ball. On a break:*)

DOG. *Switch!*

(**GOPAL** *swoops, taking the lead from* **DOG**. *Now he and* **JILL** *dance while* **DOG** *watches. The leads go back and forth this way, switching again and again on the appropriate beat,* **JILL** *deftly following one lead, then another. It's an impressive demonstration.*)

DOG. *(clapping)* That's my wife, baby!

(*On a break,* **DOG** *jumps in again.*)

DOG. Did you miss me darling?

JILL. I always miss you.

(**LYDIA** *enters and watches her parents. As the song ends,* **DOG** *dips* **JILL** *low.*)

DOG. And they lived Happily…Ever…After.

(*He kisses* **JILL***, still in the dip.*)

DOG. *(seeing Lydia)* Oh, *my* bad! No Parental PDA!

JILL. Lydia! Sweetie! Were you there the whole time? I didn't see you!

LYDIA. You guys look pretty good.

(*Rest.*

JILL *and* **DOG** *look at one another.*)

DOG. She thinks we look good.

LYDIA. Yeah.

JILL. Well thanks, honey.
So Gopal. Can you quickly go over the footwork on that first break? The bob bada THREE–

(**GOPAL** *goes over the footwork with* **JILL**.)

DOG. How's it going, cutie?

LYDIA. Fine.

DOG. You okay? You look a little flushed.

(He feels **LYDIA**'s *forehead.)*

LYDIA. I'm fine. I'm excellent.

JILL. Okay, great, so take me through one more time from the beginning...

LYDIA. Actually I wondered if I could steal the dance instructor and have a lesson right now.

(They all look at **LYDIA.**)

JILL. Really.

DOG. Honey, why don't we go to the jazz intensive.

JILL. Sure. Of course. Have a wonderful class, plum. See you tomorrow, Gopal.

GOPAL. See you.

*(***JILL & DOG*** exit.* **LYDIA** *and* **GOPAL** *look at one another.)*

LYDIA. So. You want to teach me something?

GOPAL. You been practicing?

LYDIA. Sort of. – No. Not at all.

(She's beaming.)

GOPAL. It's sort of unusual for a student to be so happy about that.

Well, hold out your arms, and let's begin.

We'll just start with some 6-count, okay?

(He leads a turn.

LYDIA *is somewhere else.)*

GOPAL. Okay...

(He leads another turn less successfully.)

GOPAL. ...You're resisting my lead.

LYDIA. What?

GOPAL. You're resisting my lead. A little resistance, good. Too much resistance, you don't get invited to dance again.

(He leads a turn. She doesn't get it.)

GOPAL. Resisting.

(He leads yet another turn less successfully.)

GOPAL. Resisting.

LYDIA. You know Gopal I'm a feminist. Maybe that's why I'm bad at this.

GOPAL. Take my word for it: feminism and swing are compatible.

But *I* lead, and *you* follow.

LYDIA. Yeah, "separate but equal."

(They dance.)

GOPAL. Now you're anticipating.

LYDIA. *Jesus!*

GOPAL. I didn't *lead* that turn. You decided to go.

LYDIA. You know, when Mr. Gonzales dances with me, he's not always telling me how lame I am.

GOPAL. Mr. Gonzales isn't your teacher.

Plus, he is not a particularly strong lead.

LYDIA. He is too. He is to me.

(They dance.)

GOPAL. There! That's it!

LYDIA. What.

GOPAL. *That's* a follow.

LYDIA. Fine.

GOPAL. See? We're dancing. I'm not trying to make you fall for a trick.

(They dance.)

GOPAL. You feel the difference? You're following.

– She's following!

LYDIA. I am?

GOPAL. Yeah. Good!

(They dance.)

LYDIA. Gopal.

GOPAL. Mm hm.

LYDIA. If I learn to follow like a dream will other people find me irresistible?

GOPAL. Just listen to the music. Follow.

*(They dance. **LYDIA** smiles, just a little.)*

scene 18
the Shim Sham.

P.A. VOICE: *Hey, cats and kittens, it's time for the Shim Sham!*

(Everyone is out on the floor for a group lesson, a swing line dance

They stand in this order:

LEAD • JILL • MR. GONZALES • LYDIA • DOG • FOLLOW • GOPAL

Everyone does the Shim Sham.

Initially **LYDIA** *and* **MR. GONZALES** *are laughing together, trying to do the steps in time.)*

LYDIA. *(to* **MR. GONZALES,** *over the music, while dancing)*
I am the shim shammer, my friend…

(Then: **JILL** *bumps* **MR. GONZALES,** *both laugh, and then they partner up and swing together, apart from the rest of the line.*

GOPAL, DOG, LEAD *and* **FOLLOW,** *and* **LYDIA** *continue the line dance – no partners.*

LYDIA *stops dancing, watching her mother and* **MR. GONZALES** *together. She stands alone and watches them dancing; they are very happy. No one notices her.*

GOPAL *and* **DOG** *and* **LEAD** *and* **FOLLOW** *continue to do the shim sham.*

JILL *and* **MR. GONZALES** *dance in a separate light than* **LYDIA.**

Lydia's face changes.)

LYDIA. Mr. Gonzales And My Mother.
Mr. Gonzales And Jill are…
They…

Mr. Gonzales And My Mother are having an affair.
Everything makes sense. No wife. Jill wanting to go to swing camp at the same time. Bringing dad is the perfect cover.

And me.

Look at them.

(**MR. GONZALES** *and* **JILL,** *who have been dancing in a non-intimate way, stop and stare at each other.*

Music changes from 'shim sham' to 'romantic.'

MR. GONZALES *and* **JILL** *begin to neck passionately, theatrically, like in the movies: Lydia's fantasy.*

Lights fade on them in a clinch.

Everyone continues the shim sham.)

scene 19

(LYDIA sits outside on the steps. Head on knees. GOPAL sitting next to her.)

GOPAL. Hey. Lydia…It's your lesson. Lindy Hop time.

LYDIA. Who the fuck cares.

Why don't you go Lindy with Jill. Everyone does.

GOPAL. What are you talking about.

LYDIA. This is the most fucking depressing place I have ever been in my whole entire life. Everyone has a partner. *Some* people have two!

GOPAL. What's the *matter*.

LYDIA. You know, my mom told me that before she married my dad, she went on a diet and ate only eggs and grapefruit for an entire year. So when she married my dad she was a perfect size four. I could NEVER eat eggs and grapefruit for a whole year!

GOPAL. So.

LYDIA. So.

She's the prettiest.

She's the best dancer.

She's been everywhere first.

And now *I* have to be *here*, at *Swing Camp* and watch her be first. Again.

GOPAL. You're a good dancer. And beautiful in a way that's all your own.

LYDIA. Why don't you say I have a charming *personality*. Jesus *God* Gopal you are depressing.

GOPAL. You've got a lot going for you Lydia. But I wouldn't put a charming personality at the top of the list.

LYDIA. Do you like my mother?

GOPAL. What. Sure.

LYDIA. I mean, do you *like* her.

GOPAL. Do I like her.

LYDIA. Yeah. Like, are you trying to get in her pants.

GOPAL. Christ.

LYDIA. Are you?

GOPAL. No. That's ludicrous. I would never.
  Do you believe me? *(simply)* No. Just no.

LYDIA. Okay.

GOPAL. Okay?

LYDIA. *Okay.*

GOPAL. So we're friends.

LYDIA. Chh. You want to be my friend.

GOPAL. Call me crazy. I do.

  (**LYDIA** *considers.*)

LYDIA. Okay. "Friend." When was the first time you had
  sex?

GOPAL. This is totally inappropriate.

LYDIA. Gopal, come ON. Talk to me. Almost nobody *talks*
  to me!! I'm just asking how *old* you were. I'm not talking about a pubic hair on my coke.

  (Rest)

GOPAL. I was fourteen.

LYDIA. God. *Everybody* did it before me.

GOPAL. Boys are idiots. Believe me.

LYDIA. So you regret it?

GOPAL. Not – It's not age that matters. Look. You're too
  smart to–

LYDIA. Everything is about sex.

GOPAL. Not always. But–

LYDIA. *(interrupting)* Shh.

  (**DOG** *and* **MR. GONZALES** *walk above.* **LYDIA**
  pulls **GOPAL** *so that they are unseen by Dog and Mr.
  Gonzales.*)

LYDIA. *(whispering)* My mother and Mr. Gonzales are having
  an affair.

GOPAL. What?

LYDIA. Jill and Mr. Gonzales are having an affair.
  I can tell.

GOPAL. I don't think so.

LYDIA. My mother and my dad are breaking up and my mother and Mr. Gonzales are having an affair.

GOPAL. Your parents don't act like people breaking up.

LYDIA. Shh.

(**DOG** *and* **MR. GONZALES** *are chatting.*)

DOG. Remember the back and forth Charleston?

MR. GONZALES. Yeah I think so.

DOG. What's the lead there, how do you get into it, is it on the three-four.

MR. GONZALES. *(counting to himself)* one-two-three-and-four...I dunno how to – let me show you.

LYDIA. *(whispering)* See. He's being extra nice to my dad. Cause he feels guilty.

(**MR. GONZALES** *and* **DOG** *begin to practice dance together.*)

LYDIA. Oh. My. God. I was wrong.

GOPAL. Well I'm glad you realize it.

LYDIA. It's not my MOTHER and Mr. Gonzales. It's my DAD and Mr. Gonzales.

(**MR. GONZALES** *and* **DOG**, *who have been dancing in a non-intimate way, stop and stare at each other.* **MR. GONZALES** *and* **DOG** *begin to neck passionately, theatrically, like in the movies. Lydia's fantasy.*)

LYDIA. Do you see that?

GOPAL. *(looking)* They're getting good.

LYDIA. They're *together!* They're going out! I have a *gay dad!* Don't you see it?

GOPAL. *(looking)* No.

(*Lights fade on them in a clinch.*

LYDIA *watches.*)

LYDIA. This camp is Fucked Up.

- act break -

act two

scene 20
somewhere (the bends)

(Blue/green light. Ocean shimmer.

Underwater. Three figures move slowly across the sandbar. Their scuba gear obscures their features.

The only sound is the dull thud of a faraway beating heart.

Bubbles rise from the mouths of the figures.

A school of silver fish streaks through the water; the figures are transfixed, watching.

Very faintly...

...a great distance away...

...we hear the tinny sound of big band music, as if being played up at the surface of the water from a transistor radio.

The underwater figures look up. Then at each other. The heartbeat speeds up.

One figure releases weights and flies up, bubbles in its wake. The other figures watch it, necks craned.

The two remaining figures look at each other. One holds out its arms. They begin to dance to the distant music, but slowly, underwater.

One figure suddenly flies upwards, leaving the last figure alone. The last figure looks up, craning its neck.

Music continues.

LIGHTS FADE.)

scene 21
now or never

(**LYDIA** *perches somewhat precariously high atop a ledge
of a wall outside the ballroom.*)

LYDIA. Mr. Gonzales: gay.

Mr. Gonzales – with my dad, not Jill.

Maybe.

(**DOG** *exits the ballroom below her, practicing.*)

DOG. One two, three-and-four, five six, sevn-and-eight.

One two, three-and-four, five six, sevn-and-eight.

LYDIA. Dad!

DOG. Oh hey, honey. What are you doing way up there?

LYDIA. Reading.

DOG. Oh. Hey, I just came from a styling workshop. Check
it out.

(*He does a move.*)

LYDIA. (*bored*) Right on.

Hey, I have to show you something.

(*She pulls out a men's skin mag and throws it down to
him.*)

DOG. *Jesus,* Lydia! Where did you get this?!

LYDIA. Paid Oliver in the kitchen to buy it for me when he
went into town.

DOG. For Christ's sake! You should not be reading this!

LYDIA. Does it turn you on?

DOG. *What?!*

LYDIA. Dad, if you're a man who loves men, it's okay.

DOG. I'm not a man who loves men!

LYDIA. Don't get homophobic about it.

DOG. I'm not – Lydia get your ass down from there!

LYDIA. Why!

DOG. Because –

(He doesn't know why.)

Never mind! – I'm taking this!

LYDIA. You can have it.

DOG. *I don't want it.* Jesus Christ on the cross!

(He stalks off. Throws the magazine violently aside.)

LYDIA. Huh.

*(**MR. GONZALES** strolls on. **LYDIA** stands up on the ledge when she sees him. He doesn't see her at first. She is far above him.)*

LYDIA. Mr. Gon-   Jack.
Jack.

MR. GONZALES. Well hello there.

*(**MR. GONZALES** looks at her. She just smiles a little goofily.)*

MR. GONZALES. And...see you.

LYDIA. I'm going to ask you a question, okay?

MR. GONZALES. *(bemused)* Ask me a question.

LYDIA. Are you gay?

MR. GONZALES. Am I...? No.

LYDIA. You're sure.

MR. GONZALES. Fairly sure.
Why do you ask?

LYDIA. Because.

(to us)

Right now, I'm looking at Mr. Gonzales, and I *see* him.
And he's looking back at me, right into my eyes, and he sees me.
And I understand that everything that's happened in my life up to now has been about preparing me for this moment, this instant of recognition. I know, I know that I am meant for him. That's all. And when you *know* something that big, you have to *do* something big. So I do. I raise my arms high, I lean forward, and I fall.

I fall from an impossible height, I fall with my back flat,
I fall through the air and even as I'm falling, I know
that I'd be really hurt, maybe killed, if I wasn't caught.
But, see, I know, I know he's going to catch me.
And he does.

(**LYDIA** *is in* **MR. GONZALES**'s *arms.*)

LYDIA. I love you.

MR. GONZALES. *Jesus!* Jesus fucking Christ!

(He drops her or puts her down roughly.)

LYDIA. I do. That's why I'm here.

MR. GONZALES. Lydia, what you just did was *crazy!* Do you
understand that? *Insane!* What if I hadn't caught you!

LYDIA. But you did.

MR. GONZALES. But what if I *hadn't.*

LYDIA. But you did.

MR. GONZALES. *Jesus!*

LYDIA. I love you.

MR. GONZALES. I'm going to pretend for your sake that you
didn't say that.

LYDIA. But I did.

MR. GONZALES. *Stop it!*

LYDIA. You danced with me. You listened to me. You told
me things. You talked to me, really talked to me. You
caught me. I want – I want...

MR. GONZALES. I have nothing to say.

No. Don't talk.

You should not have done that.

(He stalks off.)

LYDIA. But I did.

scene 22

(Dance class. **GOPAL** *stands with* **LEAD** *and* **FOLLOW**.*)*

GOPAL. Falling into a dip.

This movement is *led* by the man. But how *far* the dip goes is up to the woman.

(A comment from the class.)

Because usually the lead *is* a man.

(A comment from the class.)

Not in your case, that's true Sharon.

(A comment from the class.)

For the purpose of this class, let's assume that the follows are *women* and the leads are *men*.

(A comment from the class.)

Except for Sharon. And Emily.

My point is, the *follow* decides how Fast, and how Far to fall.

*(***GOPAL*** demonstrates.*

LEAD *dips* **FOLLOW**, *holding her parallel to the ground, and then steps away.* **FOLLOW** *stays in the exact same position.)*

You trust your partner to give you the appropriate lead.

*(***LEAD*** *and* **FOLLOW** *dance, demonstrating a low, low, dip. The follow is an inch from the floor.)*

scene 23

(**JILL** *is drinking tea.* **MR. GONZALES** *comes in.*)

MR. GONZALES. Jill. There you are.

JILL. Hi there.

MR. GONZALES. Hey. Where's Dog?

JILL. Phone call.

MR. GONZALES. Have you seen Lydia lately?

JILL. Not since this morning.
By now she's probably found a place to go get a tattoo.

MR. GONZALES. I wanted to check with you, see how she was doing...

JILL. Oh, God, has she unleashed something at y- – because she has a talent for saying exactly the most inappropriate thing, and you need to know, it's not personal, it's just: Lydia.

MR. GONZALES. Our last conversation. Took kind of a turn.

JILL. I'm sorry if she's been abrasive. Obviously you're dealing with major family issues of your own, you don't need that kind of–
God. That just came out – insanely, wrong. Jesus. Sorry.

MR. GONZALES. No. It must be obvious. I know.

JILL. Are you and Michelle talking.

MR. GONZALES. No.
You don't...think it's weird that I came here without them.

JILL. No. I don't know. Maybe. Yes.

MR. GONZALES. I just – it got bad, uh unexpectedly, and I didn't know really what to do, or. Well. So.
We're just taking some space.

JILL. Sure. No, I understand. I mean, I don't know, but. Sorry.
I feel like an asshole.

MR. GONZALES. Then stop.

JILL. All right.

MR. GONZALES. *(a wrap-up)* Things seem to happen for a reason.

(JILL nods.)

MR. GONZALES. But I just wanted to check on Lydia, with you…

JILL. She's at that age. You know.

(Little rest)

MR. GONZALES. I remember.

JILL. Do you.

MR. GONZALES. Yes.

JILL. Well you're younger than me.
There are days when I look at her, and I barely recognize…this tall person…who used to be my *baby*. It's amazing.
She's not a baby any more.

MR. GONZALES. No.
She's a remarkable young woman.

JILL. With a remarkable mouth.

MR. GONZALES. Well, she thinks something, and she says it.
…I probably don't do that often enough.

JILL. She's fearless.

MR. GONZALES. She is.
It's a wonderful trait to be around. Rare.

JILL. Listen, I'll talk to her – she can't go around just being rude anytime she feels like it.

MR. GONZALES. Oh – she's not rude.

JILL. Well she needs to be reminded to respect other people. Not to just say anything she wants to you because she thinks it's funny.

MR. GONZALES. I'd feel badly if, because of me, you said something. I mean, she hasn't done anything wrong. Don't mention anything.

JILL. All right.
And I *am* sorry about…everything.

MR. GONZALES. You're saying that a lot.

JILL. True. Sorry.

　…It's so much easier, isn't it?

MR. GONZALES. Hm.

JILL. Dancing.

MR. GONZALES. Than what.

JILL. Talking.

> **(LEAD** and **FOLLOW** *dance into the scene.* **JILL** *and* **MR. GONZALES** *watch.)*

MR. GONZALES. Maybe.

JILL. Or, just a better conversation.

> **(JILL** *exits.*

> **MR. GONZALES** *is left alone.)*

scene 24
too close for comfort

(Music. **GOPAL** *has taken* **DOG**'s *phone away. They dance together.)*

GOPAL. Don't be afraid to simply hold a moment.

DOG. How do you mean.

GOPAL. You don't always have to be moving right into the next combination. It's good to break. Listen.

DOG. And what's your partner doing?

GOPAL. She's with you. She's waiting with you.

DOG. What if she doesn't want to wait?

GOPAL. Well. You're dancing together. And you're the lead.

DOG. Right. Right.

GOPAL. So you *give* her space to do her thing. While you hold. You *give* her space, she doesn't *take* space.

DOG. Right. Right.

GOPAL. Listen. Here the music takes you high – then you can go low, then back. That's the break.

DOG. Right.

GOPAL. Here. Feel this:

*(***GOPAL*** leads ***DOG*** in some breaks.)*

DOG. Your partner knows this is going to happen?

GOPAL. My partner's waiting for my lead. We're working together, listening. To the music. To each other.

(Concentration.)

DOG. That's the trick of it, isn't it. Listening to both.

GOPAL. It is.

DOG. Huh.

GOPAL. You don't want to throw every step you know into a single dance. It's simply about your partner, and you.

(An attempt at a move.)

DOG. It's hard to stay with a partner.

GOPAL. Sometimes.

> You seem to have done all right.

DOG. Yeah.

> You know, I came here to make Jill happy. Be the best lead she'd ever have in her life. I love dancing with my wife.

> But if she *didn't* want to dance, that would be okay with me too.

GOPAL. You're a good dancer. A good lead.

> *(DOG sees Gopal's father dancing.)*

DOG. Your dad knows what he's doing.

GOPAL. These days, he mostly does the books: columns and columns of numbers. Until he hears that music. Then he straightens up, his eyes glow, and he looks around to find my mom.

> *(DOG thinks about it.)*

DOG. You know you're right, I don't break enough. In the songs. I should just stop, listen to the music. Think about what comes next.

> *(They dance again.)*

GOPAL. Listen for the break.

> *(He hums the music to highlight the break.*

> *They break...and hold...for eight beats, then start up on the same beat. DOG has been a little off the break.)*

DOG. I'll keep working at it.

scene 25
paper moon

(Dance lighting. **LYDIA** *sits alone outside the ballroom.)*

P.A. VOICE. *...and remember, tonight's After Hours Dance will take place at Pier 6, starting at midnight through the wee hours!*
(Clapping, music from far away. **GOPAL** *approaches* **LYDIA.**)

GOPAL. Lydia. You left the dance, now I have no one to Lindy with.

LYDIA. Quit being retarded, Gopal, you can dance with anybody.

GOPAL. You skipped your lesson this afternoon. I missed you.

LYDIA. You know, did you ever consider that I might be here for a reason other than dancing?

GOPAL. Sure. Scuba.

LYDIA. Other than scuba.

*(***GOPAL*** clutches his heart.)*

GOPAL. Other Than Scuba.

LYDIA. Forget it.

GOPAL. Come on. I'd like to dance with you.

LYDIA. Gopal, do you think it's possible for one person to be totally certain of something, and the other person not to get it at all?

GOPAL. Yes.
For example, I'm certain that you should follow me into the ballroom and be my partner for the next dance, and you don't get it at all.

LYDIA. What's the point.
It doesn't matter anyway. I'm never going to be good. I suck.

*(***GOPAL*** is taking off his tie.)*

LYDIA. What, you're going to *strangle* me because I ditched the fucking swing shindig?

GOPAL. We're trying something.

LYDIA. I'm *not* going inside to dance.

GOPAL. You don't have to.

(*He puts his tie around her eyes like a blindfold.*)

LYDIA. Whoa.

Okay, this is officially weird.

GOPAL. This is going to help you follow.

LYDIA. "Marco!" "Polo!" (*giggling*)

Gimme a bat, where's the pinata!?

GOPAL. Just listen to the music, smarty pants.

LYDIA. Ooh, 'smarty pants.' Trash mouth.

(**GOPAL** *takes the blindfolded* **LYDIA** *in his arms and dances a complicated Lindy with her. She follows.*)

LYDIA. So, should we–

Oh my god.

(*She dances. It takes all her concentration since it's fast.*

GOPAL *is leading advanced moves.*)

LYDIA. Jeez. *Jeez.* (*missing a step*) – Sorry.

GOPAL. No "sorry," Lydia, it's a *dance.*

LYDIA. Okay. Okay.

(*They dance beautifully, better than she's ever danced before.*

The blindfold has created a momentary magic: **LYDIA** *has become a brilliant dancer: confident, graceful, joyous.*

MR. GONZALES *has entered and is watching from afar.*

The music ends, and **LYDIA** *is laughing, spinning, thrilled.*

She doesn't take off the blindfold.)

LYDIA. Wow. Wow. Wow. This is so excellent. I feel like Luke Skywalker. You're the Obi-Wan of swing, Gopal.

(**GOPAL** *becomes aware of* **MR. GONZALES**, *who puts a finger to his lips "shush" – and motions for* **GOPAL** *to "leave, it's OK."*

GOPAL *looks at* **MR. GONZALES**, *at* **LYDIA**, *and steps away from* **LYDIA** *reluctantly.*

LYDIA *holds out her arms.*

She takes a step forward, arms outstretched, still laughing. **MR. GONZALES** *shoos* **GOPAL** *again, who begins to walk back towards the ballroom.*)

LYDIA. I'm like that blind ice skater they made that movie about.

(**MR. GONZALES** *steps up to* **LYDIA** *and takes her in his arms in a lead.*)

LYDIA. You know, the one in the 70s with Robbie Benson–

(*She stops talking when she feels the dance lead.*

MR. GONZALES *holds her for a moment, and then they dance.*

LYDIA *keeps the blindfold on.*

The dance ends with **MR. GONZALES** *holding* **LYDIA** *in a low dip. They hold this position, trembling.*

She takes the blindfold off.

MR. GONZALES *stands up and steps away from* **LYDIA**. *She takes one step towards him, another, leans forward, and kisses him.*

She stands back, looking him in the eyes.)

LYDIA. Okay.

MR. GONZALES. Okay. Okay.

(**GOPAL** *sees from far away.*)

scene 26
zip gun bop

(**DOG** *is putting shirts in a bag.* **JILL** *keeps taking them out again.*)

DOG. OK, OK, ha ha ha.

JILL. It's not funny. Stop packing.

DOG. You just *ripped* one!

JILL. That was ripped before.

DOG. No it wasn't!

Baby, come on. It's not such a big deal.

JILL. It is to me.

DOG. It's a few days. I have to take care of this.

JILL. You promised.

DOG. Jill, you're being very silly.

JILL. No *you* are.

DOG. *This is important.* Everything could fall apart if I'm not there.

JILL. I could say the same thing about here.

DOG. No you couldn't sweetie. OK cut it out with the shirts.

JILL. No.

DOG. That's pathetic.

JILL. *You're* pathetic! Can't keep a promise!

DOG. What, are you gonna call me an Indian Giver next?

JILL. *(withering)* You Didn't Give Me Anything.

DOG. I just want to get this deal over with, I want to keep my business from falling and collapsing into itself, I want to make a decent living and I want to be reasonably happy.

JILL. Why reasonably? Why not *un*reasonably? Why can't we be unreasonably happy? That's such a stupid thing to say.

DOG. *Will you stop taking my shirts out of the bag!*

JILL. *No!*

DOG. Fine. I'll go with no shirts. Because I *am* going.

JILL. I don't want you to.

DOG. That's abundantly clear.

JILL. You are *always* paying attention to your business, and not to what matters.

DOG. Sorry it doesn't matter to you. Happens to feed our family, but other than that.

JILL. We said we were going to have time away together.

DOG. We have. We are. *I'm just going to be gone a few days.*

JILL. The most amazing capacity for shortsightedness, you.

DOG. Not going to respond to that.

JILL. Of course not.

DOG. I'll miss you.

JILL. Easy. Easy to say.

DOG. Easy to say because it's true.

JILL. Well don't go and you won't miss me.

DOG. I like to miss you.

JILL. Big fucking deal.

(*A moment.*)

DOG. Right. Fine.

Can I please have a shirt.

JILL. No.

DOG. Fine. Tell Lydia goodbye, and I'll *see her in a few days.*

JILL. No.

DOG. (God.) Fine.

(**DOG** *starts to go.*)

DOG. I had been thinking up to now that dancing with you was bringing us closer. You in my arms every day. But it's not, is it.

JILL. I don't know.

DOG. Right. Me too.

(**DOG** *leaves without a bag.*

JILL *looks at the beautifully folded shirts, shakes one out, puts it on. She unfolds another, ties it around her waist. She unfolds a third shirt, tosses it over her shoulders.*

She sits wrapped in Dog's shirts, biting a nail, lost in thought.)

scene 27
the frim fram sauce

(Slow music.

GOPAL *and* **LYDIA** *dance simply.*

Too simply. **LYDIA**'s *bored.)*

LYDIA. This is kind of slow Gopal.

(GOPAL doesn't answer.)

LYDIA. Don't you want to teach me something new?

(GOPAL doesn't answer.)

LYDIA. Hey, Cowboy. Hellooo.

GOPAL. I can't dance with you right now.

(He stops.)

LYDIA. Are you mad at me?

GOPAL. Don't act dumb.

LYDIA. I'm not dumb.

GOPAL. I know. Don't act it. You are how old?

LYDIA. You know how old I am.

GOPAL. I want to hear you say it.

LYDIA. Age doesn't matter.

GOPAL. Just say it. If you asked, say, a policeman, it would matter.

LYDIA. Fourteen. I'm fourteen. I'm going to be fifteen in three months. You said you were fourteen when *you–*

GOPAL. *(cutting her off)* All *right.*

LYDIA. I'm happy. I've never been happier in my whole life.

GOPAL. It's wrong. What that man is doing is wrong. Wrong, illegal, immoral, and I wish to God I had never seen it.

(LYDIA can't really contain her joy.)

LYDIA. I love him. I've fallen in love. And he has too.
He says, he tells me, "You. Are everything. I want."

GOPAL. Yeah, he wants you, and he wants a sandwich too, because he's hungry.

LYDIA. What's that supposed to mean?

GOPAL. Life is not only about *wanting* and *having*. His behavior, forget it, it's shameful. You're a minor.

LYDIA. Gopal, it's not him. It was me: I did everything. Me. I started it. And he, he saw me.

GOPAL. I saw you. I see you. But I don't have to piss all over you to make sure you belong to no one but me.

LYDIA. I *want* to belong to him. That's the difference.

It's going to be OK.

Things work out when you fall in love. I'm OK. I am. OK.

GOPAL. Aside from being Illegal, the man is married. He has a family.

LYDIA. Most of the time, I'm all – I'm not even *here*, I'm invisible, I'm underwater and then when he touches me, I never…I…

He, he and then – I'm in my body.

Julie-Anne never described it right.

GOPAL. I have to tell your parents. Or you do.

LYDIA. You're shitting me.

GOPAL. I'm serious.

(**LYDIA** *is trembling with rage.*)

LYDIA. No you're not.

GOPAL. I am.

LYDIA. FUCK YOU. You don't understand.

GOPAL. God damn it.

I do understand. I went out with a woman who was married.

(**LYDIA** *looks at* **GOPAL.**)

LYDIA. My mother?

GOPAL. *Not your mother!*

LYDIA. *Okay. Jeez.*

GOPAL. Two years ago. I just, I couldn't help myself. – No. I decided: I allowed myself to. To do this one thing. And I got hurt. Everyone gets hurt.

LYDIA. So you know. You fell in love.

GOPAL. Lydia, are you *listening*?? Whether I fell or not isn't the point. The whole thing was a mistake! A mistake! She was married. She had a family. She had a life. And *those* are the things that endure. Not the lapse in judgment.

LYDIA. So I'm just a lapse. A fuckup. A mistake. No one could possibly fall in love with me.

GOPAL. No. No, that's–

(She is upset.

He hugs her, awkward, guilty. Holding her.

LYDIA *looks up, tries to kiss him.*

He pulls away.

LYDIA *runs off.)*

scene 28

(DOG and JILL are playing dominoes. LYDIA enters. JILL looks up absently.)

DOG. Hi sweetie. You just come from the Lindy intensive?
LYDIA. No.

Dad. Jill. I have to tell you something.
JILL. What is it honey?
LYDIA. I'm having – I'm going out with Jack.
DOG. Jack *who.*
LYDIA. Gonzales. Jack. I've been going out with Jack.

(Rest)

DOG. Okay is this some kind of joke?!
LYDIA. No.
DOG. I'm going to get very upset in a minute. I'm taking this in.
LYDIA. Dad. We're in love. I'm not kidding. I know he loves me. And his marriage is not working out. They got married too young.
DOG. *Too Young!* I am not hearing this!

LYDIA.	**JILL.**
He's 24, and I'm 14 – it's *just like you guys* – and we talked about it, and I don't want to lie to you and neither does he, because it is real.	WAIT A MINUTE, WAIT A MINUTE...!

(MR. GONZALES appears.)

MR. GONZALES. I should probably say something about now.
DOG. Oh JESUS!
JILL. *What* is going on!
MR. GONZALES. What she said.

DOG. The only reason I'm not upset yet? I'm in shock. I DON'T BELIEVE THIS! I WANT A RATIONAL EXPLANATION!	**JILL.** What are you talking about! What about Michelle?

MR. GONZALES. She's left.

> Michelle and I are still friends. We're in therapy; we'll co-parent. But the marriage is over.

LYDIA. Mom, Dad: we're in love!

> Things work out when you fall in love.   **JILL.** I don't–

> It worked out for *you.*

JILL. That's true…

MR. GONZALES. Dog, I love your daughter. She is everything I want. Try to understand.

DOG. Understand. UNDERSTAND! She's my baby.

JILL. She's not a baby anymore.

MR. GONZALES. That's right.

JILL. Well thank god Michelle left *you!*

MR. GONZALES. I know. It could have been uncomfortable.

> *(TABLEAU: think the Waltons family photo.)*

LYDIA. *(to us)* This is how I imagine it.

> **(JILL, DOG,** *and* **MR. GONZALES** *all hug, laughing and chattering.)*

LYDIA. But it's probably unrealistic. They'd be mad…

DOG. *(sudden, lunging at* **MR. GONZALES***)*
> I'M GOING TO KILL YOU, YOU
> CHILD-MOLESTING 24 YEAR OLD
> ASSWIPE! AND AFTER I KILL
> YOU, I'M GOING TO SUE YOU!
> AND AFTER I SUE YOU, I'M   **JILL.** *(holding* **DOG** *back)*
> GOING TO MAKE SURE   *FOR GOD'S SAKE!*
> YOU GO TO PRISON AND THAT   *WOULD YOU GET*
> YOU ARE THERE FOR A VERY!   *OUT OF HERE, JACK!*
> LONG! TIME! AFTER YOU'RE
> DEAD!

MR. GONZALES. *(holding Lydia's hands, speaking intensely)*
Lydia. You have to hold on for a few years. You can do anything when you're eighteen. I did. I'll leave Michelle, and the time will fly. We'll be together. I promise. *Just hold on.*

DOG. YOU'RE MEAT, GONZALES! AHH!

(*A puff of smoke, he's gone.*

A pair of shoes rests forlornly where Dog stood, tiny yellow flames dancing, smoke rising from the shoes. JILL *stares at the empty shoes in horror, turns slowly to* LYDIA.)

JILL. You killed your father.

(*She drops to her knees over the shoes and sobs.*)

LYDIA. Maybe telling them isn't such a good idea after all.

(DOG *appears again.*)

DOG. You aren't in love with my daughter, Jack. It's me you're in love with.

(*He kisses* MR. GONZALES.)

JILL. Bastard! You know you want me.

(*She kisses* MR. GONZALES. GOPAL *appears.*)

GOPAL. You are all seriously misled. Jack and I have been lovers since we were freshmen together at Cal.

MR. GONZALES. I didn't go to Cal.

GOPAL. Shut up you fool.

(*He kisses* MR. GONZALES.)

LYDIA. Hold it!

(MR. GONZALES *approaches* LYDIA, *looks into her eyes.*)

MR. GONZALES. We were meant for each other.

(LYDIA *dips* MR. GONZALES *in a swoony embrace.*

Swing music blares suddenly, loudly, but strange and warped.

DOG, JILL, GOPAL *and* MR. GONZALES *begin a wonky dance – swing gone terribly awry. Each of them swirls off, dancing wildly, jerkily.*

LYDIA *is alone.*

JILL *walks through the smoke.*)

JILL. What is it Lydia.

LYDIA. Nothing. Nothing.

(JILL *begins to exit.*)

LYDIA. Jill.

JILL. Mm hm?

LYDIA. Did you have a nice dance class this afternoon?

JILL. Very nice. You going to try West Coast Swing later?

LYDIA. No. Scuba.

JILL. Well, great. See, swing camp hasn't been so bad, has it?

LYDIA. It's okay.

JILL. Okay sweetie. I'll see you in the dining hall at dinner. Oh, your dad just called – he sends hugs. He'll be back before the big costume ball, and he said for you to save him a dance.

(**JILL** *departs.*)

LYDIA. I want to say something out loud and I don't. I don't. But it's with me all the time, this amazing secret, pumping through my blood. I keep thinking it shows on my skin.

scene 29

(Underwater.

Blue/green light. Ocean shimmer.

The **LEAD** *and* **FOLLOW** *dancers lindy through in wondrous underwater fashion, very slowly.*

LYDIA *and* **MR. GONZALES** *dance through, intimately.*

JILL *moves through the water, dragging a school of fish behind her.)*

scene 30
the spit scene/bubble of love

(**LYDIA** *and* **MR. GONZALES** *play cards. They kneel across from one another.*

Each holds half a deck of cards.

LYDIA *is euphoric.*)

LYDIA. One.

MR. GONZALES. Two.

LYDIA. Three. SPIT.

(*They proceed to play spit, a mind-bogglingly fast card game which involves each person slapping their cards down on the pile.* **LYDIA** *finishes her cards.*)

LYDIA. SPIT!

MR. GONZALES. Cheater.

LYDIA. It's sad when a person can't deal with his inadequacy. Very sad.

(**LYDIA** *kisses him. He kisses back. They neck.*)

MR. GONZALES. Again.

(**LYDIA** *kisses him again.*)

MR. GONZALES. The *game.*

LYDIA. I can't deal the cards if you don't give me my hands.

(*He releases her hands.*)

MR. GONZALES. I'm winning this time.

LYDIA. Yeah right.

(**LYDIA** *deals cards.*)

LYDIA. Ask me a question.

MR. GONZALES. Okay.

Where's your dream place to scuba dive?

LYDIA. Australia. The Great Barrier Reef. I'm going there once I get certified.

MR. GONZALES. And then you'll take me into the deep.

LYDIA. Maybe.

MR. GONZALES. Why do you like being underwater.

(Rest)

LYDIA. You can't hear anything but your breath.
You're somewhere you've never been before, ever,
and there's nothing but you and your heart.

MR. GONZALES. Sounds pretty good.

LYDIA. Yeah.

MR. GONZALES. Ask me a question.

LYDIA. Okay.
Did you get in trouble a lot when you were younger.

MR. GONZALES. No; I read all the time. I was a bookworm.
I liked to be alone. When I was around other people I
would get very quiet. I remember always being terribly,
terribly nervous that I would somehow say something
wrong. So I wouldn't talk at all. I'd just observe.

LYDIA. Huh.

MR. GONZALES. I was a strange kid. I got so good at being
quiet, people would forget I was in the room. Sometimes *I* would forget I was in the room.
Here's the difference between you and me, Lydia. No
one will ever, ever forget you're in the room.

(MR. GONZALES kisses her palm.)

LYDIA. What do you think about when we're. When you
touch me.

(Rest)

MR. GONZALES. I worry that I'm ruining your life.

LYDIA. That's *depressing.*

MR. GONZALES. It's complicated.

LYDIA. I don't think it's complicated.

(She smiles uncomplicatedly into his eyes.)

MR. GONZALES. I worry that I won't let go.

(LYDIA sees someone in the distance.)

LYDIA. Look it's Attilla from class. *Hey Attilla!*

(*They both wave.*)

LYDIA. You are not ruining my life.

Okay.

MR. GONZALES. Okay.

LYDIA. Tonight's the last night.

There's a costume ball tonight.

Are you going to the costume ball.

MR. GONZALES. Are you.

LYDIA. I wanted to know if you'd go with me. To the costume ball. Never mind. That was stupid. Never mind.

MR. GONZALES. I would like to go. With you.

But...

LYDIA. (*quickly*)

I know.

(*Rest*)

(*She smiles at him.*)

MR. GONZALES. Will you dance with me when we're there?

LYDIA. Okay. Okay.

MR. GONZALES. Okay.

scene 31

LYDIA. Last day of class. Certification dive.
Because of rain, the ocean's murky and dark.
But we do the dive anyway.

I get underwater and
something happens.

My breath is coming short and fast. My heart pounds
like crazy. I look at my depth gauge and it's *OK*, I've
been deeper than this. I've gone deeper than this. I
have.

My instructor is signaling me. *'Breathe slowly,'*
I try to make the sign with my hand that I am OK.
Because I am. OK.

And I imagine myself turning blue, about disappearing
right into the water, into nothing. And my heart beats
even faster and I try to breathe deeper but no and I
release my weight so that I fly straight to the surface.

I can't catch my breath.

You can try again next year, my instructor tells me.

I wish I could go under again, just once more.

scene 32
the costume ball

(**LEAD** *and* **FOLLOW** *move seamlessly across the ballroom floor.* **LEAD** *is dressed like 1940s doctor;* **FOLLOW** *is dressed as a WWII nurse.*

GOPAL *and* **JILL** *stand outside the ballroom at the railing, leaning, looking out at the sea.*

They are in costume: **GOPAL** *wears a bright blue zoot suit, and matching wide-brim hat.*

JILL *wears a glamorous 40s dress. She looks picture-perfect, a war bride.*

GOPAL *and* **JILL** *turn and watch inside the ballroom.*)

JILL. Your parents are wonderful dancers.

GOPAL. They are.

They've been partners a long time.

JILL. I never saw my parents dance together. They were very happy – I'm sure they were happy – but, that's what I remember most about them: that they didn't dance. So when I met Dog, when he asked me out, I told him very sternly that I wanted to take lessons, that I wanted us to *dance together.*

It was like a test.

And he said 'fine' so easily. And when we had our first lesson together – which was also our first date – he tried so hard. He really did. I felt guilty. And after that lesson, I said, okay, you don't have to come with me anymore. But he just looked at me and said, well if I keep coming with you, by the time you marry me, I'll be really good.

And he was.

GOPAL. Have you talked with Lydia?

JILL. Oh, she's heard this story a million times.

GOPAL. No. About…

JILL. Is something wrong?

GOPAL. No. No.

JILL. You're very sweet to her.

GOPAL. She's a friend.

JILL. She's this wonderful thing, my daughter.

GOPAL. She is.

Lydia makes me sad, a little–

JILL. She makes you *sad?* Why?

GOPAL. Because – she is so much *herself,* so undiluted, I just – remember what it was like to be 14. That age.

Awful and wonderful.

Riddled with doubt and knowledge.

She's so, *raw* – and.

It makes me glad not to be that age anymore.

And her age also makes me remember the sexual affair I had fallen into. When I was that age. An affair with someone older. Old enough to know better.

(Silence. **JILL** *looks at* **GOPAL**. **DOG** *enters wearing a sailor suit. He looks remarkably like the kid on the crackerjack box.* **DOG** *opens his arms.)*

DOG. Hey! Hey! Give a sailor a dance?

Who's going to dance with me first?

*(***JILL** *runs into the ballroom.)*

DOG. Um. What'd I miss? *(calling:)*

Good to see you too, honey!

Look at me. I wore this over on the god damn ferry.

GOPAL. You look good.

DOG. For Christ's sake, Gopal, I look like a refugee from On The Town.

*(***JILL** *drags* **LYDIA** *outside.*

LYDIA *is also in costume, wearing a 40s skirt with a flare and a very tight low cut top – perhaps a mink stole.)*

LYDIA. Mom what is your *problem!* Jesus Fucking Christ!

JILL. Don't talk to me that way, Lydia!

LYDIA. You just dragged me *outside!* God! That is so embarrassing!

– Dad!

(**LYDIA** *runs to* **DOG** *and hugs him.*)

DOG. Look at you, gorgeous!

(**LYDIA** *truly is remarkable – her face is made up and she looks much older.*)

JILL. I did not want to have a scene with you on the dance floor.

LYDIA. So why have a scene at all.

DOG. Honey–

JILL. Dog, be quiet!

(*to* **LYDIA**)

What are you wearing? Is that mine?

LYDIA. I just borrowed it.

JILL. That top is too old for you. Take it off.

DOG. Jill–

JILL. I mean it! Now.

LYDIA. Fine!

(**LYDIA** *takes off the top [or stole] and throws it down. She still looks lovely; sexy.*)

DOG. Lids–

JILL. You're grounded.

LYDIA. Why are you doing this? Why do you always do this!

JILL. I am not doing anything.

LYDIA. Yeah it's always me, *I'm* the problem. You know I was *dancing*. I would never grab *you* while *you* were dancing!

(**MR. GONZALES** *has come outside – he's also in a dashing costume, wearing an army captain's WWII uniform.*)

JILL. I want to know what is going on with you.

LYDIA. Nothing!

JILL. Are you having sex.

You heard me. Are you having sex.

(**LYDIA** *looks at* **GOPAL.**)

LYDIA. Yeah, Mom, I am.

> You know Attilla. Seen him in class? That's who I'm fucking.

> *(JILL slaps LYDIA.)*

DOG. *Jesus,* Jill! That's *enough!*

LYDIA. *(at GOPAL)* WHAT DID YOU SAY TO HER! WHAT!

GOPAL. Lydia, I told you I needed to say something.

DOG. Hold on a second. *(to GOPAL)* Have you touched my daughter?

> *(DOG has moved towards GOPAL.)*

GOPAL. Absolutely not. No!

LYDIA.	JILL.
Dad!	Dog!

DOG. Has everyone gone crazy? What is going on here!

MR. GONZALES. I should probably say something about now.

> *(Everyone stares.)*

LYDIA. Yeah.

JILL. Jack, this isn't your concern.

MR. GONZALES. But it is. This is something I should have said earlier. I should have done something...it's my fault. All of it.

LYDIA. No it's not.

> *(LYDIA begins to move towards MR. GONZALES.)*

MR. GONZALES. *(to Lydia)* Hold on.

> What I'm trying to say, not very successfully, is that Lydia's had, a, a, a kind of crush on me. And I was flattered – and I encouraged it. *A little. Which was wrong. But–

> *(LYDIA is frozen. She cannot believe what she has just heard.)*

GOPAL. *What did you just say?

MR. GONZALES. Excuse me, I wasn't talking to you.

GOPAL. I want to understand what you just said. Are you *blaming* Lydia? I mean, who's the adult here?

MR. GONZALES. I don't think this is any of your business.

(The following lines [*] all overlap and rise in volume.)

***GOPAL.** I don't give a care ** what you think, I'm asking you to clarify exactly what it is you're saying. Repeat it, no, really, repeat it–

***MR. GONZALES.** Look – why don't you cool down, *** and back off –

None of this has anything to do with you–

I said BACK OFF

****JILL.** Both of you, stop it–

I don't understand what you're trying to say

STOP IT

What do you mean, a crush, what's that supposed to –

STOP IT, BOTH OF YOU

*****DOG.** Hey, hey–

easy now

Gopal, what is going on here –

HEY

Cut it out – WHOA!

Back off – I'm telling you BOTH RIGHT NOW to back off–

*(During the above, **GOPAL** is getting in **MR. GONZA-LES**'s face. **MR. GONZALES** has given **GOPAL** a shove. **GOPAL** swings hard at **MR. GONZALES**, connecting with his jaw.*

A fracas.

*We might see **LEAD** and **FOLLOW** dancing in the ball-room, but slowly, as though underwater.*

***LYDIA**, shivering, climbs high atop the wall and stands above and apart from the fray.*

Music from far away.)

LYDIA. At school there was this book everybody was passing around, it was called the Magic Eye.

There are no words, only pictures. You stare at this picture, it's a picture of nothing, just a thousand dots, nothing. And then something *clicks,*

and

your eyes fall into the picture that's been there all along.

"People make mistakes."

And I see it clearly, like I never saw it before:

I am his mistake.

You can't force your eyes to see the Magic Eye Picture. You just have to wait. Wait and see.

(She raises her hands above her head, looking like a professional diver.

JILL *sees her daughter.)*

JILL. LYDIA!!

*(***LYDIA*** dives.*

Everything goes blue.

The only sound is of a faraway beating heart.

The **LEAD** *and* **FOLLOW** *dance through in their doctor/nurse costumes.)*

scene 33

(Outside an infirmary. **JILL** *sits.* **MR. GONZALES** *sits beside her. His uniform has been torn, and he has a black eye.)*

JILL. You should go. We're not going to hear anything more until morning.

MR. GONZALES. I want to be sure she's going to be okay.

JILL. You should *go.*

MR. GONZALES. I'll go when Dog comes back.

JILL. Jack – fine. Never mind.

MR. GONZALES. Listen. You heard the doctor. Lydia's going to be okay.

It's a miracle that it was high tide.

The worst thing that'll happen is that she'll have a cold.

JILL. And a crush.

MR. GONZALES. Right.

JILL. Why didn't you say something to me.

MR. GONZALES. It felt. I felt – awkward.

JILL. Because of Us.

MR. GONZALES. Yes.

JILL. Jesus.

You know, that was a long time ago, and it's long over.

MR. GONZALES. I know, and I'm telling you that I still felt awkward.

JILL. *(burning)* This, this situation infuriates me.

I don't even know how to talk to you.

You *knew* she had a crush on you?

That is crazy!

What kind of behavior is that!	**MR. GONZALES.**
And why *wouldn't* you feel	It's not any "kind" of –
awkward – I mean, God!	
What were you thinking?	

MR. GONZALES. I wasn't thinking. I wasn't – thinking anything. I just *left;* I told you.

And what was I supposed to say.

JILL. You were supposed to say, "Jill I think your daughter has a crush on me." Why am I telling you what you should have said!

MR. GONZALES. I didn't say anything to you because it felt like a betrayal.

JILL. Of whom?

MR. GONZALES. I would have felt as though I was betraying Lydia. If I had said something to you.

JILL. So you thought that quietly watching my daughter fall for you was a prudent way to handle the situation.

MR. GONZALES. I don't know what I thought! Obviously, I thought wrong.

I thought: she seemed like she needed a friend.

I liked to listen to her.

I care about her.

I never planned to hurt anyone.

JILL. Tonight I watched my daughter fall five stories, staring at you. And. If she had died. Do you know what my last words to her would have been? "That's not yours. Take it off."

(Rest)

MR. GONZALES. *(gently)* She didn't die.

You have to believe that everything is going to be okay.

JILL. Go away.

MR. GONZALES. Don't sit here and imagine the worst – why would you do that.

JILL. Because I'm her mother.

MR. GONZALES. It's not your fault.

JILL. It's my *responsibility.*

You're responsible for the people you love.

MR. GONZALES. Lydia's at that age – you said as much.

JILL. *(quiet)* I did.

(Rest)

Go. Away.

Which part don't you understand?

MR. GONZALES. I'll see you in the morning. I'm on the
morning ferry.

Tell Lydia – tell Lydia I know she's going to be okay.

(**MR. GONZALES** *leaves.*

DOG *comes out from the infirmary. His cheek is ban-
daged.*

He sits next to her.

He takes her hand and holds it.

They both look straight ahead, holding hands.)

scene 34

(**DOG** *stands with a suitcase;* **GOPAL** *stands with clip-board and sign-out stuff.*)

GOPAL. It's good you're avoiding the rush. On the ferry.

DOG. Sure.

GOPAL. You guys are on the five thirty, right?

DOG. Right.

GOPAL. That's a nice time to be on the boat. Afternoon sun.

DOG. Great, great.

GOPAL. You got all your bags okay?

DOG. Oh, sure. Yeah, we're okay.

GOPAL. I saw Lydia this morning. She looks fine.

DOG. She does. She is.

I'm sorry. For my behavior.

GOPAL. You don't owe me an—

DOG. I do, I'm saying I'm sorry. You're a good teacher. You're a good young man and I made a serious mis-judgment. I apologize. Just let me. I'm sorry.

(**GOPAL** *nods.*

He hums the same music from before to highlight a 'break.'

They break together...and hold... for eight beats, then start up on the same beat.

DOG *smiles, takes the suitcases and walks away.*)

scene 35

(**LYDIA** *sits alone on a bench. Her face is puffy, as though she's been crying.*

JILL *enters.*)

JILL. I packed for you. So we're ready to go. Next ferry.

LYDIA. Where's Dad.

JILL. He's down at the boat.

LYDIA. Where's Mr. Gonzales.

JILL. I don't know.

LYDIA. Did he say goodbye to you?

JILL. No.

LYDIA. He probably left already.

JILL. Probably.

LYDIA. Just you and me, huh.

JILL. Yes.

I'm sorry.

LYDIA. Why.

JILL. I'm sorry because...

I have had crushes before. And I remember. What it was like.

LYDIA. It wasn't a 'crush.'

JILL. I didn't pay attention. I didn't see. And you were hurt. And it's my fault.

LYDIA. No it's not.

JILL. Did he. Did Mr. Gonzales. "Encourage" you. Did he ever–

(*Silence*)

JILL. Because if I thought,

If you tell me he Did Something–

Lydia.

Because you can tell me. Please.

I don't think that I could live with myself. If that were true. Because it would be my fault. It would be my fault entirely.

You're the thing I love most.

(*Rest*)

(**LYDIA** *speaks to us.*)

LYDIA. I know – in that moment, I will never tell her.

Because it will change everything.

Because she'll hate herself.

Mostly because when you tell people things, those things – they're not yours anymore. And this will always be mine.

I'll never say anything.

It becomes my secret.

Mr. Gonzales sinks down, submerges somewhere inside me.

(Rest)

LYDIA. Mommy.

I just liked him. And it was embarrassing when he didn't like me. That's all.

It sucks though.

Are you and Dad going to–

JILL. No.

(Rest.)

JILL. You know when you were born, when I felt you coming out of my body I couldn't believe how much it hurt. That fierce pain. That endless pushing. And it made me *happy*, I was so happy because I felt you kicking, and then I saw you, so perfect, and holding you, I knew that I would take any amount of pain for you. I would.

Labor was just a fraction. I wanted it always to be that easy.

(Faint music from the ballroom.)

You are so beautiful.

What a silly thing that seems like to say right now.

But it's true.

(**JILL** stands up and holds out her hand.)

JILL. Want to dance.

LYDIA. Mommm. Gah.

JILL. I mean it.

(**JILL** continues to hold out her hand. Slowly, **LYDIA** gets up. Music.

LYDIA and **JILL** dance smoothly together.

Fade to blue.)

End Play

PROPERTY LIST

Scene one
Clothes, suitcase, jacket

Scene Three
registration desk, papers, baggage, tags ("swing passports"), papers

Scene Six
snorkeling gear, conch shell

Scene Seven
snorkeling mask, tube, book

Scene Nine
cellphone

Scene Ten
folding chair

Scene Eleven
candles (milk cartons, sand, wax) candlemaking trophy that reads "JILL!";
banner that reads "#1 CANDLEMAKER!"; lanyard materials; keychain
with 20+ lanyards on it

Scene Twelve
book

Scene Thirteen
playing cards

Scene Twenty
scuba gear, fish, bubble

Scene Twenty-One
men's skin mag

Scene Twenty-Three
tea

Scene Twenty-Four
phone

Scene Twenty-Six
shirts, suitcase

Scene Twenty-Eight
dominoes, burned pair of shoes

Scene Twenty-Nine
school offish

Scene Thirty
playing cards

Scene Thirty-Two
various vintage costumes

Scene Thirty-Three
bandages

Scene Thirty-Four
suitcase, clipboard, pen

Also by
Bridget Carpenter...

The Faculty Room

Up

Please visit our website **samuelfrench.com** for complete
descriptions and licensing information